Social Media: Dynamism, Issues, and Challenges

Social Media: Dynamism, Issues, and Challenges

Ainin Sulaiman & M Muzamil Naqshbandi

PARTRIDGE

A Penguin Random House Company

To order additional copies of this book, contact
Toll Free 800 101 2657 (Singapore)
Toll Free 1 800 81 7340 (Malaysia)
orders.singapore@partridgepublishing.com

www.partridgepublishing.com/singapore

Contents

ACKNOWLEDGEMENT

The publication of this book would not have been possible without the support, hard work, and endless efforts from those involved in the Social Network Dynamics Programme. We would like to offer our special appreciation to Professor Dr Wan Ahmad Tajuddin bin Wan Abdullah, the former dean of the Computation and Informatics Research Cluster at the University of Malaya, for providing the opportunity to form the Social Network Dynamics Programme. Thank you for believing in us.

To all the graduate research assistants, research assistants, and IPPP staff (Azrin and Melati) involved in the Social Network Dynamics Programme, our heartfelt gratitude goes to you for facilitating our research endeavours.

To all the authors, we hope this book will act as a platform. May you succeed in your future academic undertakings.

To the families of those associated with Social Network Dynamics Programme, thank you for your patience, support, and understanding, without which the chapters may not have been completed.

Finally, we would also like to acknowledge the financial support provided by University of Malaya via grant number RP004-13ICT.

PREFACE

The social-media phenomenon has changed the landscape of communication around the world. Boundaries have disappeared to a large extent, connecting people for social and official purposes. The world is now very connected and internetworked.

The main aim of this book is to present contemporary issues on social media for the general public as well as academicians, researchers, postgraduate students, and social-media practitioners. This book consists of a compilation of chapters, written by authors from various academic backgrounds, which discuss the dynamism in social media, issues, and challenges.

The content of this book is derived from research conducted on social media from various interesting perspectives. As such, it incorporates multiple approaches. The research topics span from national-level issues (such as crime detection, civic engagement, and social innovation) to individual-level issues (such as social-media usage and its impact on students). This research varied from one to two years in duration with international collaborations. The other interesting fact about this book regards the disciplines that have contributed to the discovering of social-media utilisation. Social media is widely used in current economies that require the economists, technologists, and human behaviourists and psychologists to share their perspectives on unveiling the issues and challenges. Thus, this book has been written to incorporate the multidisciplinary perspectives on the utilisation of social media.

The whole journey of this book began as a humble initiative to document research under the Social Network Dynamics programme for the Computation and Informatics research cluster of University of Malaya. In total, it combines more than thirty years of academic expertise and research experience. Upon completion of the research programme, the team for each sub-programme sat down and worked on a piece of work that could best present the outcomes of their research. Towards the end of 2013, a series of workshops were conducted during which it was noticed that there are common themes that the researchers highlighted in their research, themes which need to be shared with the people outside the academic environment and which required attention. It was also felt that there should be a mechanism to capture the current research gaps in social media. Thus, it is hoped that the findings presented in each chapter of this book would provide a platform for future researchers and practitioners to learn about the utilisation of social media and investigate them in other settings.

This book is the first book of its kind to focus on social media in Malaysia from various perspectives. It is hoped that the authors would be able to expand the chapters to provide latest trends in social media utilisation in the near future. This will enable the expansion of social media and thus, contribute to knowledge.

Finally, we hope that readers find the book helpful and interesting.

Associate Prof. Dr Che Ruhana Binti Isa

CHAPTER ONE

Introduction

M Muzamil Naqshbandi[1] and Ainin Sulaiman[1]

The advancement of information technology (IT) has led to changes in the way people conduct social interactions. This has resulted in a paradigm shift from how people communicated traditionally face to face to computer-mediated social interaction that leverages the IT advances made by humankind. In this context, computers, and more recently, handheld and allied devices have revolutionised modern communication, thereby changing the way people interact, communicate, and even think (Weisgerber and Butler 2010). At the heart of this revolution lie various types of social media including social networking sites or social network sites (SNS).

Social network sites are Web-based services that allow individuals to (1) construct a public or semi-public profile within a bounded system, (2) articulate a list of other users with whom they share a connection, and (3) view and traverse their list of connections and those made by others within the system (Boyd and Ellison 2007). One may also look

---

[1]   Department of Operation and Management Information System, Faculty of Business and Accountancy, University of Malaya, 50603 Kuala Lumpur, Malaysia.

at SNS as online communities of people who share their interests or explore interests of other members in a community. Users usually share and explore the interests using several means like chatting, messaging, e-mailing, live audio and video chatting, and more.

While computers have traditionally made SNS accessible, of late availability of handheld devices such as smartphones seems to have led to increasing use of such sites. Results of a recent survey indicate that in many countries, people use their smartphones to access social networks. The practice was particularly found to be common in Egypt (79 per cent), Mexico (74 per cent) and Greece (72 per cent) (Pew Research 2010).

While people across the world might use SNS for a wide array of reasons, five broad motivations seem to exist for the use of SNS: (1) to express deeply felt emotions; (2) to provide commentary and opinions; (3) to document the user's life experiences; (4) to articulate ideas through writing; and (5) to form and maintain community forums. The aim of information-seeking is also regarded as a factor for the use of SNS (Kim and Kim 2011).

SNS have spread across the world rapidly, leading to a user base of 1.73 billion. The rapid spread of SNS is true of the developed as well as the developing world. In countries including the UK, the United States, Russia, the Czech Republic, and Spain, about half of all adults now use SNS like Facebook and other similar websites. SNS are also popular in many lower-income nations, where people tend to use the Internet for social networking once they gain access to it (Pew Research 2010).

Most of the SNS originated in the Western world. However, given the higher population of Asia, Asia-Pacific has the largest social-network user base in absolute numbers, with an audience of 777 million people and a share of 44.8 per cent of social-network users worldwide which was expected by the end of year 2013. Forming this major user base of SNS are two Asian giants, China and India, accounting for

494 million users as of 2013. Asia-Pacific's top placement is followed by Latin America (216.9 million users), North America (181.2 million users), Western Europe (174.2 million), Central and Eastern Europe (173.6 million) and the Middle East and Africa (209.8 million) (Pew Research 2010).

The above numbers must be interpreted with caution. In 2013, 67.7 per cent of the Internet users around the world were expected to use a social network at least once a month. Out of these, a huge majority (80.5 per cent) of the Internet users in Middle East and Africa use SNS. This region is followed by Central and East Europe (74.3 per cent), Latin America (72.4 per cent), North America (66.6 per cent), Asia-Pacific (64.2 per cent), and Western Europe (61.5 per cent). While Asia-Pacific region has the most number of SNS users, it is the Middle East and African region where most of those who go online, use SNS. Surprisingly, in comparison (in percentage terms), Internet users in the Western European region use SNS less frequently than in any other region.

Although the number of people using SNS is already significant, this number is expected to increase further. According to a recent report, nearly one in four people worldwide were expected to use social networks in 2013. The number of social-network users around the world was projected to rise from 1.47 billion in 2012 to 1.73 billion 2013, an 18 per cent increase. The report predicts an even bigger user base of 2.55 billion by 2017 (*eMarketer*, April 2013).

Such a huge user base, while ambitious, may not be impossible for social-media sites to achieve. There is considerable interest in social networking, particularly amongst low- and middle-income nations. SNS, in fact, can be addictive. Not many people in the developing world have easy access to the Internet, as is the case in the developed world. However, as people in the developing countries get on the Web, they tend to use social-networking sites. Once people are online, they generally become involved in social networks at high rates. For instance, a recent survey of twenty-one nations shows that a vast majority of Internet users in developing countries such as Mexico, Brazil, Tunisia, Jordan, Egypt, Turkey, Russia, and India are using social-networking sites (Pew Research 2010). To make sense of the social media "fever", one may take the case of the rising significance of social media in some countries (such as India), where almost all the conventional media have registered their presence on the social-networking websites (Media Aid 2010). That points to the current popularity of social media and gives an indication about the future of social media.

Types of Social Media

The use of social media spans individual and organisations. Organisations in particular regularly use social media to interact with their clientele for enhanced services. Social media integrate knowledge, social interface, and content creation to collaboratively connect online information. Through social media, people or groups can generate, systematise, amend, remark on, combine, and distribute content, all to help their organisation achieve its mission or goals in a better way. Some of the most commonly used types of social media are:

Blogs: Blogs are Web pages or websites through which writers express themselves in an arrangement like a diary. Most of the successful and motivating blogs allow the authors and the readers to interact.

Social-Networking Sites (SNS): Social-networking sites (such as Facebook) offer platforms to build social networks or social relations amongst people who share interests, activities, backgrounds, or real-life connections. Such social networking are usually Web-based applications that allow individuals to connect, communicate, and collaborate with one another. Individuals create user profiles on social-networking sites that allow them to share information and join networks based on geographic location or interests (White et al. 2009).

Microblogs: Microblogging services (such as Twitter) enable users to send, read, and view comments in a concise way by limiting the characters to a certain number. Microblogs usually allow the users to read the comments without a need to register, while posting their own comments or view requires registration with the microblogging site.

Wikis: Wikis (such as Wikipedia) contain a large amount of information on a multitude of issues and topics. Users can search information on wikis in many ways based on their interest and needs. Wikis generally allow the readers to contribute after registration. Because of this, the information contained in wikis may not always be reliable. Wikis, however, are generally helpful for basic general knowledge about issued related to varied walks of life.

Video Portals: Video portals (such as YouTube) are sites that allow watching of video through their online applications. Besides allowing the users to watch video based on their needs and tastes, such sites let users to upload their videos for sharing with the entire world. Some video portals also allow live streaming of events, which can be watched in real time by viewers across the world.

Discussion Forums: Discussion forums are websites that allow users to discuss any kind of issues, post their reviews of products, share their experiences about products, services, and places, and virtually anything under the sun. Many individuals, organisations, and associations use discussion forums to propagate their ideology and counter their opponents. These discussion forums provide useful information and opportunities for readers to get updated on a specific topics and issues. Usually, discussion forums have several sections that users can access depending on their interests.

In addition to the above types of social media, there are also websites that allow users to store and share their photos, such as Flickr. Flickr allows its users to share and embed personal photos and at the same time, provides an option to bloggers to host images that they embed in blogs and social media.

Social Media: Who use them?

Social media have captured the fancy of people from all walks of life, people who use them for different purposes and interests. Below are the few main user categories of social media.

a. Youth

Energetic and educated youth all over the world are considered to be both the main target audience and user population of social-media networks. A recent study conducted on the usage of social media reported that people below thirty years of age comprise the main population engaged in social-media activities, and they are also on the top for using smartphones to access social media. This trend of accessing social media using handheld devices indicates that youth in particular want to stay in frequent and constant touch with other people across the world. Along similar lines, Reda et al. (2012) report that the agewise distribution of most of the social-networking members from across the world is naturally skewed towards people of younger age. Another report revealed that the young people were more involved in using smartphones to access social-media sites, as compared to their counterparts people with age of above fifty (Pew Research 2010).

b. Students

Over the years, social media have become popular amongst college students. It is a way to make connections, not only on campus, but with friends outside of school. Social networking helps many people feel as though they belong to a community (Choney 2010). There is a survey of twenty-one countries regarding the use of social media for positive purposes such as education. The survey, conducted by Pew Research Center, revealed that the approach differs in terms of education by which people use their cell phones. Respondents with a college education were observed to be at least 10 per cent points more likely to know about using the Internet on mobile phones as compared to those without a college degree. In addition, these results offer a clear picture of the use of social media for educational purpose. This trend is increasing day by day. As a result, many top universities around the world have started programmes regarding research and implementation of social media for educational purposes.

c. Politicians

The use of social media by politicians has seen an upward trend, even in developing countries. Political parties try to reach out to the masses using different types of social media. Whilst the role of social media by politicians in the developed world is well known (for instance, in the last elections in the United States), politicians in developing countries like Malaysia, Pakistan, and India have also leveraged social media to put across their messages to the people. In some countries, major as well as minor political party members have opened accounts on Twitter, Facebook, and the like. In the days before social media, journalists carried the messages of the political leader to the people. Due to the advent of social media, political leaders are now increasingly communicating to the people directly through more direct online channels. Users, on the other hand, use social media progressively, as they too want to have awareness of causes, be a part of campaigns they relate to, and participate in discussions on common issues using these platforms (Australian Broadcasting Corporation, 30 July 2013).

Use of social media to get support for some specific cause or bill to be opposed or supported by the public is very common nowadays. Social media can be useful for organising large numbers of individuals quickly (Bong, et al. 2012). Civil society and educated classes are frequently using these networks for support. In recent times, to oppose the Trans-Pacific Partnership (TPP) agreement, several social-media sites became increasingly active in many countries for the best interests of the public. The coordination of both online public protests and other events requiring in-person participation is easier now, due to the use of social media. Similarly, the extent of influence of social media on the day-to-day life of citizens and the political situation in general can be gauged through the example of recent revolutions in Egypt and other Arab nations, where several dictators were deposed. Social-media outlets can help measure public opinion of government behaviour and help anticipate public uprising for any specific issue or decision. In 2011, social media played significant roles in organising and energising many social-change movements, such as the Arab Spring, the Occupy Wall Street Movement, and the 2011–12 anti-corruption movement in India (Bong, et al. 2012). **Tourists**

As in many other industries, the role and use of social media has increased in the tourism industry too. Travellers now increasingly rely on social media to chart out their travel plans by collecting information about the places they would like to visit. Research suggests that social media comprises an extensive part of the search results, which shows that search engines most probably direct travellers to social-media sites. According to Xiang and Gretzel (2010), this authenticates the growing significance of social media in the online tourism sphere.

d. Patients

Increasingly, social media is used to gather information related to identifying, preventing, and treating different diseases, as well as connecting with healthcare professionals. Many countries now promote their medical tourism using social media. This trend is not only increasing competition in the healthcare sector, it also results in better awareness and services for patients.

Social Media: What people use them for and how?

A survey conducted by the Pew Research Centre revealed that public figures globally shared their views online about a variety of topics, especially famous culture. Twenty of the nations surveyed in this opinion poll reported that on average, 67 per cent of social-network users like to share their opinions about music and movies when they use social-networking sites, and a noteworthy number of those users also posted their views on all issues regarding community, politics, religion, and sports.

Across twenty of the nations surveyed, a median of only 34 per cent posted their political opinions. Amongst those using social-networking sites, sharing views about music and movies was a popular activity. Majorities in seventeen surveyed countries reported being involved in this activity of sharing opinions about movies, music, art, and other issues.

In the Middle Eastern region, it was found common to express one's view on issues relating to community, politics, religion, and sports. More than 70 per cent users of social-networking sites in these countries had posted their views about community issues, and at least 60 per cent had shared their views about politics (Pew Research 2010). On the other hand, social media users in the United States and Europe were found to use their smartphones to search for information about customer products, jobs, or about current affairs. More than 40 per cent of surveyed users reported that they search for products, 30 per cent said they search for jobs, and another 30 per cent search for politics or current affairs.

Advantages and Disadvantages of Social Media

The pervasive use of social media comes with both advantages and disadvantages, some of which are highlighted throughout this chapter. However, there have been continued debates amongst scholars about whether the virtual world leads to a positive or negative approach to social interaction (Totterdell, Holman, and Hukin 2008). Notwithstanding, given the relative infancy of the issue at hand, the extent to which social-networking sites enhance or obstruct social well-being of the users in terms of various facets of interpersonal relations deserves further research before inferences are made.

Of late, research has started to emerge about social-networking sites and their potentially adverse effects on psychosocial well-being (Mazer and Ledbetter 2011). Other areas of research have focused more on the regular access of social-networking sites and their effect on relational well-being (Ledbetter, et al. 2011). In addition, due to the increased popularity of social media, economists and professors are questioning whether grades of students are being affected by how much time is being spent on these sites (Choney 2010). Further, with the increasing popularity of smartphones with the capacity to run several social-networking applications, many are concerned about how this phenomenon will affect students' grades (Stollak, et al. 2011).

Other disadvantages of social media include the opportunity for hackers to carry out cybercrimes and data and identity theft. Unchecked use of social media on the part of employees of an organisation can also result in loss of productivity, especially if employees are busy updating their profiles and chatting unnecessarily.

Future of Social Media

Many users access social media with their handheld devices like smartphones, while the majority uses the traditional desktops and laptops. A survey found that in a large majority of the countries surveyed, only about 40 per cent of the respondents regularly use their mobile phone to access the social-media sites. In the future, therefore, as use of Internet on phones becomes extensive, more and more users are expected to log on to social media via their handheld devices. This process can further be expected to take place expeditiously as technologies such as mobile devices become cheaper and more people join the bandwagon. In addition, the speedily intensifying social-network listeners in the emerging markets of Asia-Pacific, the Middle East, and Africa are predicted to be the emerging drivers of social-user growth. Though Asia-Pacific is estimated to have the largest social-network population worldwide through 2017 and the Middle East and Africa the second-largest audience starting year 2014, their population penetration rates are amongst the lowest (*eMarketer* April 2013). In the future, the reduction in prices of technology can be expected to increase penetration rates amongst the people in these regions.

Conclusion

One can foretell that social media is going to shape the future of the Internet and give a new look to the global community, realising the concept of this world as a "global village". Rapidly increasing technologies and advancements in the software and mobile phone technologies are leading towards enhanced usage of social media in the world. Like mobile phones, we can foresee that uneducated and underprivileged classes of the society may also be able to interact on various social media. This entails certain pragmatic challenges for the research scholars and industry practitioners as well as civil society advocates; this emerging increase in the use of social media should be diverted towards positive outcomes for the society in general. There exists a need for different stakeholders to work together and put under control the evils such as cybercrime, identity theft etc. that pillion the use of social media. This book thus comes at an opportune time, highlighting the dynamic nature, issues, and challenges associated with social media.

In chapter two, *Mining Social Media for Crime Detection,* Kasturi Dewi and her co-author discuss the use of social media for crime detection. The chapter also focuses on suicide (which is considered as a crime in many countries) and how data mining the social media can help in preventing suicides.

In chapter three, *Impact, Issues, and Challenges of Facebook Usage amongst Students,* Nor Liyana and her co-author review literature on the impact of Facebook use by students. They show that the popularity of Facebook for higher-education students has both negative and positive impacts. Amongst the impacts cited by the authors are academic performance and personal well-being (such as self-esteem or satisfaction in life). At the end of the chapter, the authors propose several considerations for future researchers.

In chapter four, *Social Media for Civic Engagement amongst Youths,* Noor Ismawati et al. focus on how social media can be used for civic engagement, the individual or collective involvement in social issues that encompasses a variety of political and non-political activities. The authors discuss how civic engagement can be enhanced by using social media.

In chapter five, *Social Media for Social Advances: Use of Social Media in Educating Future Generations,* Farah Dina et al. shift the focus to the educational aspect of social media. They look at the Malaysian school system and highlight two educational issues and four challenges related to successful technology integration. With its cost-effective and easy-to-use features, the authors argue that social media can provide promising educational tools that can result in instructional improvement.

In chapter six, *Impression Management: Managing Followers' Impressions about Leaders' Effectiveness through Social Media,* Sharmila et al. write about the issue of impression management with respect to social media. Peppered with salient facts, figures, and examples, this chapter focuses on how leaders from around the world use social media for impression management. The authors conclude by highlighting the issues and challenges associated with leaders' impression management through social media.

In discussing social media, one has to consider the theories related to it. One of the prominent theories in the area is the media richness theory, or MRT. In chapter seven, *Media Richness Theory for Social Media Research: Opportunities and Challenges,* Noor Akma and her co-author provide a comprehensive explanation of MRT and variables that lead to media choice and media use. The authors also identify several issues, including perception and actual communication performance, dynamic, and the evolutionary nature of the media and media choice and process. The authors end the chapter by highlighting the challenges these issues create.

In chapter eight, *Social Innovation through Social Media*, Shamsul and his co-author focus on social innovation through social media. The authors argue that social innovation through social media is an area that has remained largely unexplored, although many groups of people have undertaken initiatives that fall under the concept. Using two examples from Malaysia, they highlight relatively successful social innovations and the associated challenges that need to be overcome for the success of these social innovations.

In chapter nine, *Appropriating Value from Social Media: Issues and Challenges,* Sharan Kaur et al. look at the good and the bad of social media. The authors show that social media has its own set of rules; if the user community members sense that they are being controlled commercially, they might post adverse reviews, leading to loss of repeat and potential customers, causing considerable harm to the business. To appropriate value from social media, the authors highlight several strategies that business implement and identify issues and challenges using the different types of social media and the use of strategies carried out by organisations while appropriating value from social media.

In chapter ten, *Challenges Facing Modeling the Spread of Infectious Diseases in the Community and Congregate Settings,* Noor Azina et al. discuss the practical dynamics of social networks. They authors look at demographic networking modelling of the spread of infectious diseases within communities, towns, districts, cities, regions, and the whole country (better known as the physical or traditional social network). These models may then be useful for extracting parameter values for exposure, susceptibility, and infection that can be used in future preventative strategies. The authors also discuss the issues and challenges involved in the modelling process.

References

Australian Broadcasting Corporation (2013). "Is social media Changing the Way Politics Works?" Accessed 15 September 2013 at: *http://www.abc.net.au/local/audio/2013/07/30/3814292.htm.*

Bong, S, et al. (2012). "Analysing Social Media Momentum: India's 2011–12 Anticorruption Movement". Madison, Wis.: La Follette School of Public Affairs, University of Wisconsin.

Boyd, D, and N B Ellison (2007). "Social Network Sites: Definition, History, and Scholarship". *Journal of Computer-Mediated Communication,* 13 (1), 210–230.

Choney, Suzanne (2010). "Facebook Use Can Lower Grades by 20 Percent, Study Says". *nbcnews.com.* Retrieved 1 June 2014 from *http://www.nbcnews.com/id/39038581/ns/technology_and_science-back_to_school/t/facebook-use-can-lower-grades-percent-study-says/#.UsoClvu5_GY.*

eMarketer (2013). "Worldwide Social Network Users: 2013 Forecast and Comparative Estimates". Accessed 15 September 2013 from *http://www.emarketer.com.*

Kim, S-B, and D-Y Kim (2011). "Travel Information Search *Behaviour* and Social Networking Sites: The Case of US College Students".

Ledbetter, A M, et al. (2011). "Attitudes Toward Online Social Connection and Self-Disclosure as Predictors of Facebook Communication and Relational Closeness". *Communication Research,* 38 (1), 27–53.

Mazer, J P and A M Ledbetter (2011). "Online Communication Attitudes as Predictors of Problematic Internet Use and Well-Being Outcomes". Unpublished manuscript, available at *www.media.wix.com.*

Pew Research (2010). "Social Networking Popular Across Globe: Arab Publics Most Likely to Express Political Views Online". *Pew Research*

Global Attitudes Project. Accesed on 15 September 2013 at *http://www. pewglobal.org/2012/12/12/social-networking-popular-across-globe/.*

Reda, A, et al. (2012). *Social Networking in Developing Regions*. Paper presented at the International Conference on Information and Communication Technologies and Development, Atlanta, Georgia.

Stollak, M J, Vandenberg, A, Burklund, A, and S Weiss (2011). *Getting Social: The Impact of Social Networking Usage on Grades Among College Students*. Paper presented at the Proceedings of ASBBS Annual Conference, Las Vegas, Nevada.

Totterdell, P, Holman, D, and A Hukin (2008). "Social Networkers: Measuring and Examining Individual Differences in Propensity to Connect with Others". *Social Networks,* 30 (4), 283–296.

Weisgerber, C, and S Butler (2010). "Editor's Introduction: Special Issue on Communication Pedagogy in the Age of Social Media". *Electronic Journal of Communication,* 20 (1–2), 1.

Xiang, Z and U Gretzel (2010). "Role of Social Media in Online Travel Information Search". *Tourism Management,* 31 (2), 179–188.

CHAPTER TWO

Mining Social Media for Crime Detection

Kasturi Dewi Varathan[1] and Mohammed Ali[1]

Summary: The popularity and the proliferation of social media have created massive social interaction amongst the users, which generated huge amounts of social data. Social media allow their users to easily interact and share information, thereby enhancing social interaction through the social-media sites. Through the use of targeted data-mining technologies and techniques to identify crimes from user-generated data posted in social media (for example, to identify those most at risk to commit suicide), social media can also be used for crime- detection and prevention purposes.

[1] Department of Information Systems, Faculty of Computer Science and Information Technology, University of Malaya, 50603 Kuala Lumpur, Malaysia.

Introduction

In recent years, the online user population has experienced impressive growth; there are now hundreds of millions of users across the globe. By discarding physical boundaries and enabling people with common interests to freely interact and share their ideas, emotions, and contacts, it has become a powerful means of communication that has changed the way we interact. With the existence of huge amounts of user-generated data, social media has become a fertile platform for a variety of research efforts. Current research has gone to the extent of using social-media data in predicting election results and identifying current trends in the stock market. Many researchers have ventured into social-media research, since there exist many unique opportunities that can be looked into.

Many different social-media technologies exist, such as blogs, forums, microblogging, and wikis, to name but a few. Mosley (2012) has indicated that there are more than nine hundred social-media sites available on the Internet. Of these, Facebook, Twitter, and YouTube enjoy the highest popularity ratings. Facebook produces more than a petabyte of data per day, Twitter transmits approximately 110 million tweets per day, and YouTube receives an average of more than 2 billion viewers every day (Mosley 2012).

Millions of people are interacting through Twitter, which has the highest user base on record. "Tweets" – real-time, user-generated messages of no more than 140 characters – are popular amongst users, especially younger ones, as a quick means of communication on any and all topics.

In recent crises, such as the Egyptian Revolution, Twitter played an important role as an effective and efficient medium of communication that enabled people to share information in a timely manner. Twitter was also reported to have more than 200 million users (*www.*

washingtonpost.com, 2013). Through the careful analysis and proper utilisation of such a huge amount of data available on social media, crimes could be theoretically be identified in advance and prevented.

Importance of Topic

This research focuses on the crime of suicide. After the Suicide Act of 1961, suicide is now considered a crime in many parts of the world, including Malaysia. Suicide has been reported as one of the top ten leading causes of death in the world. The number of people who commit suicide is increasing day to day, with the most (73 per cent) suicides occurring in developed countries. This toll is very worrying. In Malaysia, the suicide rate is estimated to be 1.3 to every 100,000 people (*Star* newspaper, June 2012).

Meanwhile, statistics have shown that suicide is endemic within the teenage population. According to Neal's 2012 semi-annual survey on youth risk behaviour in United States, one in every twelve teens has attempted suicide; 2011 research by Chen *et al* revealed that 70 per cent of teenagers use social-media sites every day, and almost 25 per cent of them make more than ten visits per day. John, et al. (2010) has also revealed that 86 per cent of users between the ages of eighteen and twenty-nine access social media on a daily basis. According to Naaman, Boase, and Lai (2010), 50 per cent of total messages posted by each individual on Twitter are about themselves. In many cases, suicide victims left messages on social media regarding their problems, as well as intentions of ending their lives.

Statistics have shown that around sixty-four suicide-related comments are posted within a month period in MySpace (dailymail.uk-newspaper). Suicidal young people tend to display red-flag behaviours – feelings of hopelessness, talking about wanting to die or kill oneself, or having no reason to live – on social media in the final hours before they intend to take action. Because the posted messages were not taken seriously or a suicide note was unattended, some could not be saved.

In many cases, suicide is preventable. If peer communities can be trained to recognize the warning signs of sincere intention, lives may be saved. Unfortunately, given the huge amount of data in existence, reading and identifying suicide-related messages from each and every posted messages is neither practical nor possible. It is also a very time-intensive process. Some social-media users feel no obligation to help others or prevent suicide. The mindset that "someone else" will take care of these potential suicide victims may also be to blame. In order to prevent suicides, effective and efficient identification and prevention measures need to be in place. Thus, the research is focused on methods of detecting those most at risk of attempting and finding way to prevent these at-risk users from committing lethal self-harm.

Focus of the Chapter

One-fourth of the world population is engaging and spending a significant amount of time in generating content in social media. Many businesses and researchers are taking advantage of this user-generated content. The main focus of this chapter is to identify and discuss the issues and challenges that lie behind detecting crime in social media. A study by Ohio State University also has suggested that researchers should utilise social-media sites in preventing suicide amongst teenagers (Collis 2013). The social-media application that will be discussed in this chapter is based on Twitter. The chapter will give a clear understanding of the issues and challenges in utilising services such as Twitter to identify risk and prevent suicide.

Issues

Large Volume of Data

The majority of the world's population accesses social-media sites daily. They are not only viewing the data that is available in it; each individual is spending a significant amount of time communicating and sharing their thoughts, opinions, and emotions online. This has resulted in a staggering growth in the amount of data available via social media. As of December 2010, 110 million tweets were sent every day (Mosley 2012). This has raised information-management issues as to the proper storage technique needed to store and handle these data.

As more and more people are attracted to this social-media application, the huge amount and the distribution challenges of such dynamic data generated is continuously evolving. Scalability of data growth is an important aspect that needs to be looked upon in identifying potential suicide attempts. Since it is impractical to use only historical data in identifying potential victims, this aspect is done in real time, and the technique used should be flexible enough to allow for data growth to occur in the future.

Privacy and Security

Because social-media applications enable collaboration and the sharing of information, privacy and security have become major concerns. The opposing needs of users have to be taken into account as well. There are times when the user wishes to share his or her thoughts and emotions freely, with the intention that the posted tweets will be viewed and followed by others. On the other hand, these same people are also safeguarding their information. They would not want their posts to be seen or used by other authorities for analysis or investigation purposes. The use of available information on social media without the user's consent has become a critical issue. Investigations on these data are done without the need of a search warrant. Many times, users are unaware that their posts have been used for certain investigation or analysis purposes.

"What you say is what you are" is very well suited for Twitter users. Because tweets are available to the whole globe with just a single click of a button, Twitter's terms and conditions warn their users to only post if they are comfortable with that level of exposure. Many users have not heeded this warning and have found that their own tweets have been used against themselves. These could be partly because of naivety amongst the users; too many have learned the power of the network when a seemingly innocent comment or image is used against them – and they are powerless to do anything about it.

An issue on retrieving user's tweets arises when a user's Twitter account is set as private. If the user chooses the private setting, posted tweets are not searchable or viewable without the permission of the account holder. In privacy mode, it is impossible to mine tweets or messages.

Data Retrieval

Visualisation of data is an issue that needs serious attention. Since the Twitter data pool is huge, it would be good if this data can be visualised based on the preferences so that users will be able to interpret it well. For example, if an individual's tweets can be represented as a graph indicating the total number of negative-emotion tweets on each day for the whole month, such an objective, visual representation could serve as a valuable tool in the effort to track negative tweets over a given time period. This information is crucial in identifying those at risk of suicide.

Time

The most important issue that needs to be tackled wisely in detecting and preventing suicide from happening is a timely response. Any delay in detection is potentially disastrous; the information is only useful if it is discovered and acted upon in a timely manner. Data has to be mined, indexed, and analysed in an efficient manner. The recompilation and reorganisation of data has to be given serious thought, as it takes a significant amount of processing time.

Accuracy

Authenticity, fidelity, and accuracy of user information are very important issues in mining social media (Chu 2012). Determining the accuracy and reliability of the source of the extracted suicide-related data is a serious concern; fake Twitter IDs have been used to post undesirable content. Another challenge lies in differentiating between content that is related to suicide posted by a user with no intention to self-harm and those who do intend to commit suicide. Can aggressive analysis efforts help to prevent the worst-case scenario, as one played out in England in January 2011? At that time, a woman in England posted a suicide note on her Facebook wall. She had 1,048 friends, but while her friends discussed the *legitimacy* of the post, not one came to her aid. She was found dead the next morning (Hutchison 2011).

Gender

There is also a gender issue that needs to be taken into consideration. Females are more prone to share their feelings openly, compared to males (Thelwall, et al. 2010). They have a greater ability to express emotions. Because males are not as open in communicating their feelings, it is hard to judge when one needs help.

Detecting the Right Emotions

Since the research is based on text mining of Twitter messages, a challenge lies in detecting the right emotions from the short tweets that had been posted by the users. Identifying sentiment through text alone is difficult at best because of the lack of reliable visual, audio, or body-language expressions. In this kind of circumstance, there is an increased chance that the posted message will be misinterpreted.

There are also some tweet messages that have several different meanings. For instance, a tweet such as "The End" could mean many different things, depending on how it is used. The challenge lies in accurately interpreting any such clues within available context; no small task.

Challenges

Data Challenges - Large Volume of Data Challenge

Social media can be described as a structure that enables the exchange and dissemination of information. It enables the social interaction between individuals that creates huge volumes of data; analysing such dynamic interaction is a challenging problem. For example, Twitter has 200 million active users who send 400 million tweets per day (*www.washingtonpost.com* 2013). An attempt to mine such huge and unstructured data is a big challenge for the analysts; analysing the structure and the data of social network can be performed using techniques such as that introduced by (Bader and Madduri

2006; Madduri, Ediger, Jiang, Bader, and Chavarria-Miranda 2009) but computation complexity is main drawback of these techniques. However, more efficient methods must be improved for analysing unstructured and constantly changing data.

Another challenge for the analysts is applying data pre-processing techniques to a large volume of inconsistently presented data. For example, consider the suicidal tweet below, presented exactly as it was posted:

"Tonight I want to dei, sorry every1, bye"

Because of typographical errors/deliberate misspellings ("dei") or shorthand ("every1") used, this sort of statement could easily confound any detection efforts. This illustrates one of the many challenges presented to any data-cleansing or mining efforts.

Semantic Challenges

The omnipresent use of social-media abbreviations and social-media slang will make analysing the content quite difficult. Reproducing the conversation so it could be understood is equally challenging.

Such recovery of content is important for the detection of suicide attempts. The number of Twitter abbreviations – DAM ("Don't annoy me"), DP ("profile picture"), HAGN ("Have a good night"), NSFW ("Not safe for work"), YKWIM ("You know what I mean"), and OOMF ("One of my friends/followers) changes as the medium evolves (socialmediatoday 2012).

Analysts should be aware of these abbreviations, since a suicidal person may use abbreviations to express his intention to commit suicide. A suicidal user might also use acronyms such as DIAF ("Die in a fire") to express extreme anger with a person or about an idea, or FTL ("For the Loss"). The opposite of FTW ("For the win"), FTL is a quick way to show disappointment or dissatisfaction.

Twitter slang maybe used express the early signs of suicidal intent, so researchers should understand the different slang used in Twitter in order to have effective detection of suicide.

Non-Text Data

Social media enables the use of non-text contents in the form of videos, audio, and images; therefore conventional data-mining techniques are inefficient in retrieving content. On Twitter, instead of communicating with text, a depressed person may post a photo or a video to express his or her intentions. In these cases, proper and accurate analysis of such content is technically very challenging.

Another challenge in mining social media for crime detection is data storage. Storage of huge volumes of social-media data must be considered while mining social media for crime detection, because In social-media the volumes of data increases at a faster rate than computing resources and CPU speeds. For example, the number of Twitter users and volume of tweets creates scalability challenges for the storage of streaming data. Centralised storage is not very practical; because of the large number of tweets, the data must be continuously updated. To solve this problem, innovative hardware and software solutions are required.

Privacy Challenges

The last few years have seen great growth in the social media in terms of services and users. Many social media boast millions of registered users. For example, Twitter reported 37,033,000 visitors using personal computers and 22,620,000 using mobile applications (Insights 2012). Many twitter users keep their profile private which limits the number of users be studied.

The aim of mining Twitter for suicide detection is to discover new and useful knowledge from Twitter messages. Sometimes, the messages contain sensitive information. Hence, mining Twitter for suicide detection while honouring the individual user's right to privacy is a challenge. The visibility of user profiles is necessary and an important factor in social media to introduce the users to new people. On the other hand, users invite attacks such as reputation slander or spamming when they modify privacy settings from private to public (Hogben 2007). Because of this threat, Twitter users avoid this by changing their privacy setting to private instead of public. In Twitter, the posts of users who opt for privacy will only be available for selected people. These tweets will not be available publicly, complicating any effort to detect suicide intentions.

Time Challenges

One of the greatest challenges in mining Twitter for suicide detection is in gaining timely access to intention. The timing of a suicidal tweet is a challenge, especially with dynamic and huge user-generated data. Detecting suicidal tweets and other warning signs of suicide intention promptly could help in the prevention of suicide.

For example, consider Ashley Billasano, an eighteen-year-old girl who posted 144 tweets before she committed suicide. From the content of her tweets, it was apparent that she needed someone to talk to. She was reaching out for someone to help her. More than five hundred people were following her Twitter account when she tweeted, "I'd love to hear what you have to say but I won't be around." Her last tweet, "Take two. I hope I get this right" was posted shortly before she committed suicide by suffocation (FoxNews 2011).

It can be posited that if the right people had seen the classic warning signs of suicide in Ashley Billasano's attempts to communicate, she may have received the help and support she was requesting from her friends and family. Suicide prevention is an extremely time-sensitive endeavour; a few minutes could make a change and save a life. Therein lies the core challenge: how to develop a proper technique to detect warning signs quickly enough to save a life. Early and accurate detection of the warning signs, followed by notification of concerns to the family, friends, and healthcare providers, may assist in the efforts to provide those at risk with more positive solutions.

Another time challenge in mining Twitter for suicide detection is the ephemeral nature of content; data may appear and disappear over time, making productive analysis of Twitter data in a timely fashion a challenge (Bourqui, et al. 2009).

Techniques Challenge

Many techniques, including association rules, classification, clustering, etc. exist. Choosing the most effective technique for data mining Twitter remains a subject of debate.

Association Rule

Association rule is a straightforward data-mining technique. We make relation/associations between two things, often of the same type, to identify patterns. For example, when detecting suicide tweets, we might identify that some suicidal people might mention feeling lonely when they talk about suicide.

Previous studies (such as Mosley Jr 2012) discuss several calculations that are made as part of an association analysis to determine the strength of relationships. The support is a measure of how often items occur together. This technique can be applied to mine Twitter for suicide detection, but it is efficient only for text mining. It is not applicable for non-text tweets, a challenging problem when attempting to mine Twitter data.

Clustering

By examining one or more attributes, we can collect data and make an opinion. Clustering is useful to identify and organize data into clusters, each cluster has similar features. Clustering can be applied to build an opinion structure while mining Twitter for suicide-detection data.

The clustering algorithms used in Sharifi, et al. (B. Sharifi, Hutton, and Kalita 2010) were fairly basic; they need more improvement. Before running the algorithm, a specific number of clusters is generated and must be determined. An arbitrary number of clusters should be selected to create a set of tweets, regardless of distribution of those tweets. To improve the overall experience for Twitter users and Twitter researchers, more effective algorithms and techniques are required.

Framework Creation Challenges

Large-scale social media structure and data can be analysed using theories and new concepts based on mathematical models (Malik and Malik 2011). A new framework is needed to check the validity of the theories; previous studies (Yao 2003) proposed a three-layered conceptual framework for data mining.

1. The philosophy layer (understanding): The philosophy layer discusses about the basic of knowledge, such as presentation of knowledge and organisation of knowledge. This layer is to understand the main objective of the mining social-media. A problem definition is established clearly stating its goals, and strategies. Primary data was collected from social media for the purpose of detecting the suicide.

2. The technique layer (discovery): The technique layer discusses about discovery of the knowledge how to discover knowledge. This layer selects data mining techniques that are to be employed in the study. An appropriate technique for the database is selected and maybe, more than one technique is applied to meet the goals of mining social media.

3. The application layer (utilisation of knowledge): This layer focus on the aim of the discovery knowledge and the usefulness of the knowledge. In this layer the framework is evaluated to check whether it meets all the required parameters, objectives, and to monitor if any aspect is left unattended with respect to the pre-established goals.

Twitter is a dynamic, constantly evolving service. As a result, a multidimensional framework must be developed. This is a big challenge. As the complexity of the analysis algorithms grows, it will become necessary to regularly test and check the algorithm for accuracy and scalability.

Location Challenges

A *location* is a new object in location-based social networks (Traynor and Curran 2012). In Twitter, the user location can be obtained by using API search. API responses will contain populated "geo" objects, as shown below.

```
1.  "geo": {
2.  "coordinates": [
3.  10.6115,
4.  -21.9757
5.  ],
6.  "type": "Point"
7.  },
```

All geolocation information begins as location coordinates (latitude and longitude). By using this information, the location of the user who posted a tweet can be determined. But not all tweets have a location attached, an ability that is controlled by the user's privacy settings. If a suicidal user's tweets are public, this feature can be used to find the location of the person who just tweeted his or her intentions, a crucial factor in being able to respond quickly and effectively to the threat. Location can be used to dispatch help, including response by police, medical teams, mental healthcare professionals, and others. The challenges include determining how to efficiently make use of user-generated location content and locating the at-risk user when privacy settings prevent such a disclosure.

Evaluation Challenges

In the evaluation phase, the model is analysed to determine if it meets all the required parameters and objectives and to monitor if any aspect is left unattended with respect to the pre-established goals (e.g., mining Twitter for suicide-detection purposes). But the deficiency in complete access to social-network systems such as Twitter for the validation of results is a big challenge. The challenge arises in using the information obtained to accurately identify the right potential suicide victim on time. Visualisation is needed to make the data more understandable, so we can detect unknown community clusters in Twitter. Researchers could use tools such as Vizster or Maltego to visualise trends, but as these tools were not designed for Twitter, they suffer from scalability challenges.

Other Challenges

Accuracy and Trustworthiness of the Information

Ensuring that the information that has been extracted from Twitter is accurate and true is difficult. For example, if a Twitter user posted about a desire to commit suicide, it's difficult to determine if the post reflects serious intention or not. The *Toronto Star* reported that a fan of singer Ariana Grande posted a number tweets threatening to kill herself, including "I'll take pills and I'll kill myself", and that she would end her life in three minutes. A concerned nurse in Toronto alerted the police, who took this threat seriously. Once Twitter agreed to provide the user's IP address, the police determined that the tweet originated in Greece. Although it appears Ariana Grande had no clue what took place, the fan was trying apparently to promote Grande's upcoming studio album by tweeting false alarm suicide tweets. Thus accuracy and trustworthiness of the information remain critical challenges. It is very important for the researchers to consider the source of the data in the interpretation of the results.

Representation of Database Challenges

Database representation in social media is a major challenge, as the social media is dynamic and data evolves over time (Aggarwal and Abdelzaher 2011). Database challenges are common in such massive, real-time applications. For example, a huge number of tweets may be collected simultaneously, so the ability to compress, process, and store it in real-time is useful.

Language Challenges

Twitter is a global phenomenon. Tweets are posted in hundreds of languages, further complicating data-mining and analysis efforts. Each language requires a separate initial analysis. Before analysis can be effective, accurate translations, including sentiment and emotion, would be necessary.

Conclusion

Social media produces an enormous quantity of data. There are many challenges in mining this vast quantity of unstructured and inconsistent data. Issues and challenges related to mining Twitter for suicide detection and prevention have been discussed. This discussion will act as a foundation in driving researchers to address the social-media challenges in their future research.

Tools and policies need to be developed to ensure privacy integrity will be maintained, regardless of how the data is aggregated and analysed. The protection of privacy is likely to remain a challenge for data mining in social media. Important areas that need to be addressed include longitudinal studies that can be used to inform and validate not only new data-mining technologies, methodologies, and applications, but also can help enhance our understanding of social media itself from a broader perspective. Understanding the limits of data mining is important to anyone applying data mining to social media.

There exist opportunities for productive collaborations between computer scientists, social scientists, law-enforcement specialists, and other interested authorities to use data-mining technologies and techniques to reveal patterns in Twitter data that would not otherwise be visible to detect and prevent suicide. Data-mining technologies are expected to help quantify results and provide meaningful insights. As the number of social-media users continues to grow, it is likely continue to see significant changes in the way people communicate and share information. Research will continue in order to provide the users with the empowering ability to look deeper into these large data sets in more meaningful ways.

References

Aggarwal, C C and T Abdelzaher (2011). "Integrating Sensors and Social Networks". *Social Network Data Analytics*. Springer (379–412).

Bader, D A and K Madduri (2006). *Designing Multithreaded Algorithms for Breadth-First Search and ST-Connectivity on the Cray MTA-2*. Paper presented at the International Conference on Parallel Processing, 2006.

Bourqui, R, et al. (2009). *Detecting Structural Changes and Command Hierarchies in Dynamic Social Networks*. Paper presented at the International Conference on Advances in Social Network Analysis and Mining, 2009.

Chen, Y, Zhou, Y, Zhu, S, and H Xu (2012). "Detecting Offensive Language in Social Media to Protect Adolescent Online Safety. Privacy, Security, Risk, and Trust (PASSAT)", 2012 International Conference on Social Computing (SocialCom), 71–80.

Collis, H (2013). "Could Social Networking PREVENT Teenage Suicide? Study Finds Most Young People Would Turn to Technology to Ask for Help". *http://www.dailymail.co.uk/health/article-2348602/Could-social-networking-PREVENT-suicide-teenagers-Study-finds-young-people-turn-technology-ask-help.html*.

FoxNews. (2011). "High School Girl Tweets 144 Times Before Committing Suicide".

Hogben, G (2007). "Security Issues and Recommendations for Online Social Networks". ENISA position paper (1).

Hutchison, P. (2011) "Facebook 'Friends' Mock 'Suicide' of Woman Who Posted Goodbye Message". *The Daily Telegraph* (2011 January 6).

Insights, G, Media + Entertainment. Nielsen. Retrieved 9 December 2012. "State of the Media: The Social Media Report 2012".

Madduri, K, et al. (2009). *A Faster Parallel Algorithm and Efficient Multithreaded Implementations for Evaluating Betweenness Centrality on Massive Datasets*. Paper presented at the International Symposium on Parallel and Distributed Processing, 2009.

Neal M (2012). "1 in 12 Teens Have Attempted Suicide: Report". *http:// www.nydailynews.com/life-style/health/1-12-teens-attempted-suicide-report-article-1.1092622#ixzz2hnekvkLE.*

Mosley Jr, R C (2012). *Social Media Analytics: Data Mining Applied to Insurance Twitter Posts*. Paper presented at the Casualty Actuarial Society E-Forum, Winter 2012 Volume 2.

Sharifi, B P (2010). *Automatic Microblog Classification and Summarisation*. University of Colorado.

Sharifi, B, Hutton, M-A, and J K Kalita (2010). *Experiments in Microblog Summarisation*. Paper presented at the IEEE Second International Conference on Social Computing (SocialCom), 2010.

Socialmediatoday (2012). "Top Twitter Abbreviations You Need to Know".(Accessed October 2,2013).

Thelwall, M, Wilkinson, D, and S Uppal (2010). "Data Mining Emotion in Social Network Communication: Gender Differences in MySpace". *Journal of the American Society for Information Science and Technology* 61(1): 190–199.

Traynor, D and K Curran (2012). "Location-Based Social Networks". *From Government to E-governance: Public Administration in the Digital Age,* 243.

Washington Post (2013). "Twitter Turns 7: Users Send Over 400 Million Tweets per Day".

Yao, Y Y (2003). *A Step Toward the Foundations of Data Mining*. Paper presented at AeroSense 2003.

CHAPTER THREE

Impact, Issues, and Challenges of Facebook Usage amongst Students

Nor Liyana Mohd Shuib[1] and Ainin Sulaiman[2]

Summary: Facebook is currently the most popular social-media venue amongst higher-education students. It has become an essential part of student life. Facebook use has consequently impacted students' lives, especially with regards to academic performance and behaviour. Questions about the impact of Facebook use on these areas need to be addressed. This chapter will identify the issues and challenges faced by students and researchers on Facebook usage. The purpose of this chapter is to present a review of published empirical studies focussing on the impact of Facebook use by students, with the aim of summarising the various findings. Educators and researchers could then use this information to identify unanswered issues or questions in literature, and define future research directions concerning the use of Facebook.

[1] Department of Information System, Faculty of Computer Science and Information Technology Building, University of Malaya, 50603 Kuala Lumpur, Malaysia.
[2] Department of Operation and Management Information System, Faculty of Business and Accountancy, University of Malaya, 50603 Kuala Lumpur, Malaysia.

Introduction

Social media are technology systems related to collaboration and community. The most popular social media amongst higher-education students is Facebook (Cheung, Chiu, and Lee 2011; Golub and Miloloža 2010; Hargittai 2008). Facebook was initially developed to allow students to create and maintain social ties between college and university students in different residence halls (Wikipedia 2010). Facebook was launched as a social networking site on February 24, 2004, by Harvard students Mark Zuckerberg, Dustin Moskovitz, and Chris Hughes. Users of Facebook can create a personal profile, add other users as friends, and send and receive messages that include automatic notifications when they update their profile.

Even though Facebook users are now coming from different types of educational background higher-education students are still the most prevalent users (Ellison, et al., 2007, Altaany and Jassim, 2013, Haq and Chand, 2012According to Hew (2011), motives for using Facebook include meeting new people, maintaining existing relationships, disseminating information, communicating with others, expressing oneself, and being entertained, as well as serving as task-management and educational tools. Activities on Facebook include sending messages, posting messages on a wall, updating statuses, sharing links, viewing and updating profiles, playing games, using applications, and storing pictures. Joinson (2008) reported that viewing and uploading pictures and status updates are two of the most popular activities conducted by higher-education students.

Students also use Facebook for academic purposes to complete their projects and discuss material (Haq and Chand 2012). Bosch (2009) conducted a research on fifty undergraduate students at a university in South Africa and found that they used Facebook to communicate with friends regarding academic matters, such as sharing information and learning materials and finding answers about assignment details from their Facebook friends. Even though there are claims that using Facebook can help students engage in learning, education-related activities on Facebook are still not widely used (Hew 2011). Altaany and Jassim (2013) showed that only 29 per cent use Facebook for academic purposes.

Since the use of Facebook has become a phenomenon amongst higher-education students, its use undoubtedly has some impact on them (Kirschner and Karpinski 2010). This chapter will identify the issues and challenges faced by higher-education students using Facebook. The purpose of this chapter is to present a review of published empirical studies, focussing on the impact of Facebook use by students, with the aim of summarising the various findings.

Issues

Facebook can have both positive and negative impacts on a higher-education student's academic life and behaviour. In this chapter, we will discuss the impact or issues on higher-education students, in terms of academic performance and behaviour, such as self-esteem and addiction. Several main issues are included within this domain.

Academic Performance

Much research has been conducted into the relationship of Facebook with higher-education students' academic performance. Previous research has shown that Facebook has a negative impact on students (Kolek and Saunders 2008). Kirschner and Karpinski (2010) reported that Facebook users have lower mean GPAs than non-Facebook users.

However, 79 per cent of their respondents claimed that Facebook did not have an impact on their academic performance.

Haq and Chand (2012) conducted a survey to study students' opinions about the impact of Facebook on their academic performance; 61 per cent of the respondents admitted that Facebook use had a negative impact on their academic performance. This was in line with Ketari and Khanum (2013), who revealed that 55 per cent of their respondents believed that Facebook use could have a negative impact on their grades.

Karpinski and Duberstein (2009) conducted a survey of 219 students at Ohio State University and found that Facebook users had an average GPA of between 3.0 and 3.5. Meanwhile, non-users' GPAs were between 3.5 and 4.0. They claimed that even though students stated that Facebook use didn't have a negative impact, the results showed that they had lower grades. However, because of a lack of data, they did not conclude that there was a positive raw correlation between Facebook and lower grades.

Even though research has reported that Facebook use had a negative impact on students, empirical research shows that there is a significant negative relationship between Facebook use and academic performance (Kolek and Saunders 2008). In discussing this issue, other factors, such as time spent on Facebook, activities conducted on Facebook, and multitasking should also be considered.

In discussing time spent on Facebook, most students claimed to use Facebook at least once a day (Kittinger, et al. 2012), while 65 per cent of student Facebook users accessed it several times a day (Khan 2009). The time spent varied from several minutes to more than one hour on Facebook (Hew 2011). This was in line with results from Ross, et al. (2009), which showed that the majority of respondents spent between ten and sixty minutes on Facebook daily.

In the study by Kirschner and Karpinski (2010), students who used Facebook reported spending fewer hours per week studying on average than non-Facebook users. Yu, et al. (2010) reported that students logged on to Facebook four times a day and spent sixty to ninety minutes on average per day. Karpinski and Duberstein (2009) compared study times between Facebook users and non-Facebook users; Facebook users spend about five hours a week studying, while non-users spend eleven to fifteen hours per week studying.

There has been inconclusive evidence on the impact of Facebook usage on academic performance. Some studies have reported no impact while others found there is an impact. For example, Khan (2009) found seventy-nine per cent of students using Facebook believed that the time spent on the site had no impact on their academic performance. This was supported by Lopez (2011), who conducted a survey on 1,839 undergraduates and found no real evidence that spending time on Facebook would lower students' grades. On the other hand, Kirschner and Karpinski (2010), Ogedebe, et al. (2012) and Haq and Chand (2012), Paul, Baker, and Cochran (2012) all reported that the more activity and time spent on Facebook, the lower the academic performance of the student. In other words, the less time spent on Facebook, the better the academic performance (Altaany and Jassim 2013). Ketari and Khanum (2013) reported that Facebook users had lower grades and spent less time studying than non-Facebook users. This conclusion was based on the assumption that Facebook use was carried out while studying.

Junco (2012) also showed that more time spent on Facebook had a negative correlation with the grade-point average of students. In his report, Junco (2012) reported that Facebook could not be criticised for the lower grades of higher-education students. It actually depends on the student's activities on Facebook. In his previous research, he found that students who are active on Facebook (such as those who frequently post status updates) tend to have lower grades, while those students who just check the status of Facebook and share links, tended to have higher grades (Junco 2011).

Junco's 2012 study to identify the relationship between Facebook use and grades found that there was no relationship between them. Golub, et al. (2010) reported that students' perceived negative impact of Facebook on their academic performance was found to be positively related to their Facebook use, such as for long-time use and multitasking.

Research by Jackson (2008) showed that multitasking increases mental work and that multitasking will never be as effective or efficient as doing one thing at a time. Mayer and Moreno (2003) claimed that multitasking impacts the learning process through a form of information overload and split-attention effect. By actively multitasking with both Facebook and studying, students study time is interrupted by Facebook activities, especially non-academic activities (e.g., playing games, tagging photos, and looking at video links). These results are in line with previous studies that show that multitasking activities with Facebook will negatively impact students' academic performance (Mayer and Moreno 2003).

Golub, et al. (2010) also reported that a positive impact on academic performance can be expected if Facebook is used for academic purposes. From Junco's 2011 and 2012 research, we can conclude that academic performance actually depends on how students use Facebook. If students use it for academic purposes, Facebook can actually help increase their grades. However, if students use it without control and become distracted, then it becomes a problem to their studies. This is in line with Golub, et al. (2010), who reported that negative impact to academic performance of higher-education students was positively related to Facebook usage.

Behaviour

Self-esteem is a behaviour variable impacted with the use of Facebook. Fisher (2012) claimed that the number of friends, likes, and comments on Facebook can directly impact students' self-esteem. Golub, et al. (2010) conducted a survey on Facebook and self-esteem using Rosenberg's Self-Esteem Scale. They claimed that there was a positive relationship between self-esteem and the frequency of using Facebook to communicate with friends. By using Facebook to communicate with friends, students' self-esteem can be increased. This was supported by Yu, et al. (2010), who suggested that students' self-esteem and satisfaction can be led to a higher level when they use Facebook as a communication medium to obtain information, knowledge, social acceptance, and support from friends and lecturers. Ellison, et al. (2007) also reported that Facebook can help in building self-esteem. Students with low self-esteem can gain more benefit from Facebook use, in terms of making friends and connecting with others (Ljepava, et al. 2013). In terms of academic performance, Golub, et al. (2010) reported that there was a positive relationship between self-esteem and academic performance.

Frequent use of Facebook leads to Internet addiction. Other terms for Internet addiction include *excessive Internet use* and *problematic Internet use*. Pempek, et al. (2009) reported that Internet addiction is a common topic relating to Facebook use. Khan (2009) found that 65 per cent of Facebook users accessed their accounts several times daily, while Karpinski and Duberstein (2009) reported that students spent an average of thirty-one hours online each week. These findings supported the results from Jones, et al. (2009), who compared higher-education students with the general population of the United States. They found that higher-education students are heavy Internet users.

Kittinger, et al. (2012) used an Internet addiction test to investigate the relationship between Facebook use and Internet addiction. Their findings showed that one in six students experienced problems such as Internet addiction. These findings were consistent with Andreassen, et al. (2012). As more students become Facebook users, further research is necessary to study the relationship between Facebook use, Internet addiction, and the impact to students' academic performance.

Challenges

The first challenge was sampling. Most previously published studies involved a relatively small sample, in which research was limited to one institution or demographic. Therefore, results could not be generalised to students at other institutions or demographics. Another sampling issue involved the statistical methods used to analyse the data. The use of Likert or ordinal data can be difficult to use and interpret in many statistical analyses (Kirschner and Karpinski 2010). Skues, et al. (2012) reported that many researchers did not use an appropriate statistical method.

The second challenge involved data-collection methods. Most studies used quantitative methods, such as surveys and questionnaires, to collect data. Even though these methods are effective and widely used, they often state flawed proxies for behavioural measures (Carrell and Willmington 1996). Another important challenge was to provide a standard variable that could be used by all researchers; this was supported by Kirschner and Karpinski (2010). Previous studies used various constructs for the same variable in their studies. It is hard to compare one research finding to another. For example, for the "time spent" variable, some researchers based their studies on Facebook time logged on, while others used weekly use.

Another challenge involves the study of Facebook time spent multitasking. Previous researchers only focused on the frequency of Facebook use and did not observe the actual activities conducted by students while using Facebook (Junco 2011). Different activities produce different results.

Conclusion

The purpose of this chapter was to present a review of published empirical studies focussing on the impact of Facebook use by students, with the aim of summarising the various findings. The popularity of Facebook for higher-education students has both negative and positive impacts.

Many researchers suggest that Facebook use has impacted students' academic performance negatively, but no empirical evidence exists. Other research has shown that when used for non-academic activities, Facebook use leads to lower grades, while students performing academic activities online are positively impacted. In discussing the impact of Facebook on academic performance, other variables, such as time spent and usage of Facebook, should be discussed.

Only a few studies have focused on behaviour issues, such as self-esteem and Internet addiction. A student's self-esteem was predicted to improve with the use of Facebook. Using Facebook to communicate can boost a student's self-esteem, especially for students with low confidence levels in life. Another issue is Internet addiction. Using Facebook for long periods of time can lead to Internet addiction, a distraction for students. More research is needed to address these issues, particularly Internet addiction for Facebook users only. Both variables can be related to academic performance.

Future research, specifically on students' Facebook usage impact, should be conducted.

- Researchers can explore more qualitative methods, such as observation, longitudinal study, and interviews, along with quantitative methods.
- In order to capture a broader sample, sampling methods need to be extended to allow for accurate and meaningful comparison amongst students from different institutions, countries, and demographics.
- The use of more sophisticated data-analysis techniques, such as the structural equation method (Jenkins-Guarnieri, et al. 2012), is needed.
- A verified standard survey or questionnaire that can be applied to various samples needs to be developed to help researchers to compare studies.
- Kirschner and Karpinski (2010) suggested study on students' extracurricular activities. Students who are active in extracurricular studies may have different affect results.

Educators and researchers could use this information to identify unanswered issues or questions in literature and define future research directions concerning higher-education students' Facebook usage.

References

Altaany, F H, and F A Jassim (2013). "Impact of Facebook Usage on Undergraduate Students' Performance in Irbid National University: Case Study", 3(4), 255–260.

Andreassen, C S, et al. (2012). "Development of a Facebook Addiction Scale". *Psychological Reports*, 110, 501–517.

Carrell, L J, and S C Willmington (1996). "A Comparison of Self-Report and Performance Data in Assessing Speaking and Listening Competence". *Communication Reports*, 9(2), 185–191.

Cheung, C M K, Chiu, P, and M K O Lee (2011). "Computers in Human Behavior Online Social Networks: Why Do Students Use Facebook?" *Computers in Human Behavior,* 27(4), 1337–1343. doi:10.1016/j.chb.2010.07.028.

Ellison, N B, Steinfeld, C, and C Lampe (2007). "The Benefits of Facebook 'Friends': Social Capital and College Students' Use of Online Social Network Sites". *Journal of Computer-Mediated Communication*, 12, 1143–1168.

Fisher, C (2012). "The Negative Effects of Facebook and Its Impact on Future Generations". Retrieved 15 September 2013 from *http://curtisfisher4.blogspot.com/2012/10/the-negative-effects-of-facebook-and.html.*

Golub, T L, and M Miloloža (2010). "Facebook, Academic Performnace, Multitasking and Self Esteem". Retrieved 15 September 2013 from *http://bib.irb.hr/datoteka/511252.facebook_academic_performance_multitasking_and_self-esteem.pdf.*

Haq, A, and S Chand (2012). "Pattern of Facebook Usage and its Impact on Academic Performance of University Students: A Gender-Based Comparison". 34(2), 19–28.

Hargittai, E (2008). "Whose Space? Differences Among Users and Non-Users of Social Network Sites". *Journal of Computer-Mediated Communication*, 13, 276–297.

Hew, K F (2011). "Students' and Teachers' Use of Facebook". *Computers in Human Behavior,* 27, 662–676. doi:10.1016/j.chb.2010.11.020.

Jackson, M (2008). *Distracted: The Erosion of Attention and the Coming Dark Age.* Amherst, NY: Prometheus.

Jenkins-Guarnieri, M A, Wright, S L, and L M Hudiburgh (2012). "The Relationships Among Attachment Style, Personality Traits, Interpersonal Competency, And Facebook Use". *Journal of Applied Developmental Psychology,* 33(6), 294–301. doi:10.1016/j. appdev.2012.08.001.

Joinson, A N (2008). "Looking at, Looking up or Keeping up with People? Motives and Use of Facebook". *SIGCHI,* 1027–1036.

Jones, S, Johnson-Yale, C, Millermaier, S, and F S Pérez (2009). "Everyday Life, Online: US College Students' Use of the Internet". *First Monday,* 14(10). Retrieved from *http://firstmonday.org/ojs/ index.php/fm/article/view/2649/2301.*

Junco, R (2011). "The Relationship between Frequency of Facebook Use, Participation in Facebook Activities, and Student Engagement". *Computers and Education,* 58(1), 162–171. doi:10.1016/j.compedu. 2011.08.004

Karpinski, A C, and A Duberstein (2009). *A Description of Facebook Use and Academic Performance among Undergraduate and Graduate Students.* San Diego, Calif.: American Educational Research Association.

Ketari, L M and M A Khanum (2013). "Impact of Facebook Usage on the Academic Grades: A Case Study", 5(1), 44–48.

Khan, U (2009). "Facebook Students Underachieve in Exams". *Daily Telegraph.* Retrieved 15 September 2013 from *http://www.*

telegraph.co.uk/education/educationnews/5145243/Facebook-students-underachieve-in-exams.html.

Kirschner, P A and A C Karpinski (2010). "Facebook and Academic Performance". *Computers in Human Behavior,* 26, 1237–1245. doi:10.1016/j.chb.2010.03.024.

Kittinger, R, Correia, C J, PhD, and J G Irons (2012). "Relationship Between Facebook Use and Problematic Internet Use among College Students". *Cyberpsychology, Behavior, and Social Networking,*15(6), 324–327. doi:10.1089/cyber.2010.0410.

Kolek, E and D Saunders (2008). "Online Disclosure: An Empirical Examination of Undergraduate Facebook Profiles". *NASPA Journal,* 45(1), 1–25.

Ljepava, N, et al. (2013). "Personality and Social Characteristics of Facebook Non-Users and Frequent Users". *Computers in Human Behavior,* 29(4), 1602–1607. doi:10.1016/j.chb.2013.01.026.

Lopez, V B (2011). "Time on Facebook (Kind Of) Helps (and Really Doesn't Hurt) Your GPA". *USA Today College.* Retrieved 15 September 2013 from *http://www.usatodayeducate.com/staging/index.php/ccp/facebook-helps-student-grades-study-says.*

Mayer, R E, and R Moreno (2003). "Nine Ways to Reduce Cognitive Load in Multimedia Learning". *Educational Psychologist,* 38(1), 43–52.

Ogedebe, P M, Emmanuel, J A, and Y Muse (2012). "A Survey on Facebook and Academic Performance in Nigeria Universities". *International Journal of Engineering Research and Applications,* 2(4), 788–797.

Paul, J A, Baker, H M, and J D Cochran (2012). "Effect of Online Social Networking on Student Academic Performance". *Computers in Human Behavior,* 28(6), 2117–2127. doi:10.1016/j.chb.2012.06.016.

Pempek, T, Yermolayeva, Y, and S Calvert (2009). "College Students' Social Networking Experiences on Facebook". *Journal of Applied Developmental Psychology,* (30), 227–238.

Ross, C, et al. (2009). "Personality and Motivations Associated with Facebook Use". *Computers in Human Behavior,* 25(2), 578–586. doi:10.1016/j.chb.2008.12.024.

Skues, J L, Williams, B, and L Wise (2012). "The Effects of Personality Traits, Self-Esteem, Loneliness, and Narcissism on Facebook Use among University Students". *Computers in Human Behavior,* 28(6), 2414–2419. doi:10.1016/j.chb.2012.07.012.

Yu, A Y, Wen, S, Vogel, D, and R C Kwok (2010). "Can Learning Be Virtually Boosted? An Investigation of Online Social Networking Impacts". *Computers and Education,* 55(4), 1494–1503. doi:10.1016/j.compedu.2010.06.015.

CHAPTER FOUR

Social Media for Civic Engagement amongst Youths

Noor Ismawati Jaafar,[1] Anne Marie Warren[1] and Ainin Sulaiman[1]

Summary: With the increase of social problems such as crime and disengagement from social and civic matters, democracy and public involvement in social issues are in many ways more vital than ever before. With the advent of social media, activists and advocacy groups proliferate, allowing formerly undervoiced individuals or marginalised groups to enjoy the new opportunities that Web 2.0 brings. Social media empowers the ordinary to be heard on a large scale. However, freedom of speech and postings come with worrisome trends. Also, despite the advancement of technology's ability to connect the world, many studies still report that users – in particular, youth – are being drawn away from involvement with community affairs. Civic deficit amongst youth remains at large as a problem. This chapter introduces

---

[1]   Department of Operation and Management Information System, Faculty of Business and Accountancy, University of Malaya, 50603 Kuala Lumpur, Malaysia.

briefly what civic engagement is about, the different forms it takes on, and the issues and challenges faced by youth.

Introduction to Civic Engagement

A diversity of definitions and civic forms constitute the term *civic engagement* (Putnam 2000; Ramakrishnan and Baldassare 2004; Verba, Scholzman, and Brady 1995; Weissberg 2005). *Civic engagement* refers to individual or collective involvement in social issues. Civic engagement encompasses a variety of forms of political and non-political activities. Common forms of civic engagement include making donations, participating in community work like cleaning the environment, voting, attending community meetings or functions, contributing ideas to social causes, contacting public officials, attending protests and speeches, signing petitions, serving local organisations, and writing articles concerning community matters. Table 1 shows the types of activities that are commonly associated with civic engagement and their descriptions.

Table 1: Forms of Civic Engagement

Category	Description
Volunteering/ community service	Offline or online sharing of time and/or skills (but not money)
Voting	Participation in electoral activity including voter registration, unofficial "straw polls", or other voting simulations, both online or offline
Global issues/ international understanding	Collaborative online activities that involve youth from different nations or focus on international issues

Online youth journalism/media production	Online news reporting, arts projects, documentaries, etc., that allow youth to use the Web to analyse and comment on the world
Tolerance and diversity	Activities that foster acceptance and celebration of diverse cultures, races, ethnicities, religions, sexual preferences, and body types and appearances
Positive youth development	Activities that prepare youth to be responsible individuals, including character-building and fostering of civic virtue, fostering a respect for the law, patriotism, fostering good judgment, leadership training, and ethical behaviour (including responsible Internet use)
Youth activism	Activities that help youths organise and express their political views to or about major institutions (government, corporations, schools, the media, churches, etc.), online or offline, alone or collectively, with peers or adults
Media literacy	Analysis of media representations of issues, critical thinking about media, and ethical usage of media ("netiquette", avoiding copyright infringement, surfing safely, etc.)
Workings of government	Fostering understanding of how the levels and agencies of government function (e.g., how a bill becomes law)

Social Media for Civic Engagement

Social media has been used to spotlight and highlight issues by the government, albeit limited. It is used in many ways: alerting the public to social problems, mobilising the online community to search for missing persons, or applying pressure to organisations and businesses to be more responsible in assuring the public's safety, to name just a few examples. Malaysians form the world's seventeenth-largest community of Facebook users. Because a number of online discussions and activities revolve around social issues, social media seems to be an avenue for citizens to be involved in addressing these issues. Facebook thereby presents an opportunity for users to be more civically engaged.

While there is promising evidence that people are adopting social media for civic engagement, research on citizen civic behaviours and social capital in the social-media context remains limited (Pasek, et al. 2009; Valenzuela, et al. 2009). Moreover, future research challenges social-media providers to develop a richer measure of social-media use for understanding civic behaviours (Zhang, et al. 2010); what promotes citizens' online civic engagement (Shneiderman, et al. 2011; Gil de Zúñiga 2012); and more importantly, what will lead to greater citizen trust in institutions, including the government (Bannister, et al. 2011; Parent, et al 2005).

One way of addressing social problems is by using social media to create awareness and educate the public. There are social-media studies in tailoring health communications and promotions (Buis 2011; Liang and Scammon 2011; Ahmed, et al. 2010; Avery, et al. 2010) and to combat the spread of HIV (Devan, et al. 2012). Social media empowers users to spread social causes and change perspectives and participate in digital activism. Research on social media on societal-level issues has addressed politics and government (Baumgartner and Morris 2010); for better reach, relevancy, and engagement in India (Rajapat 2009); on e-democracy in the United States (Nam 2011); for justice and democracy (Ali 2011; Choudhary, et al. 2012) and labour unions (Bryson, et al. 2011; Zachary 2011) in Egypt. One civic website, *TakingITGlobal.org,* a prominent social network with over 5 million visitors from around the world, spurs civic engagement (Raynes-Goldie and Walker 2008) and has been successful in creating relationships while addressing global issues. In these studies, social media is often seen as a vehicle for driving social change for the betterment of society. There are many events taking place online which contribute to creating social change around the world. Forms of activism on the Internet include posting civic messages and signing online petitions.

However, the scant research on civic websites for youths, as well as studies of civic-related sites for all ages, suggests that these sites have been slow to take full advantage of the medium's potential for interactivity in ways that might further boost engagement. These studies have found that sites support especially low levels of interpersonal interactivity, compared to content interactivity. For example, Montgomery, Gottlieb-Robles, and Larson (2004) conducted a study that identified and categorised over three hundred sites aimed at involving American youth in a broad range of civic activities. Although this study did not systematically define or count the number of interactive features on these sites, it concluded that many of the sites were more likely to offer information about organisations and opportunities for offline engagement (so-called "brochureware") than to provide online activities that directly train youth in civic skills or allow for participation via the Internet.

The researchers note that "most civic Web sites make minimal use if any of games, quizzes, simulations, collaborative-learning projects, and other activities that tap the Internet's capacity for interaction" (p. 128). Youth voting sites may be more interactive than other civic sites for youth. Studies of twenty-two sites designed to boost voting amongst youth in the 2002 election (Bennett and Xenos 2004) and thirty-five such sites in the 2004 elections (Bennett and Xenos 2005) found an increase in the percentage of sites offering information about voter registration, offline political events, and other opportunities for participation, as well as interpersonally interactive features such as message boards, blogs, interactive polls, and the ability to submit one's own links. Yet, even in 2004, fewer than 55 per cent of youth voting sites included any of these interactive abilities.

More precisely, the online activities amongst youth could include activism, which according to Denning (2000), is "the use of the Internet in support of an agenda or cause". This includes online actions like setting up websites, surfing the Web for information, posting materials on a website, transmitting electronic publications and letters through e-mail, and using the Internet to discuss issues, form coalitions, and coordinate activities. Based on these explanations, this study deems *online civic engagement* and *Internet activism* to be synonymous. Denning's (2000) five modes of Internet activism include: collection of information, publication of information, dialogue, coordinating action, and lobbying decision-makers.

Youth Online Civic Engagement Activities

In the collection mode of Denning's (2000) work, the Internet was used like a large online library to browse for information. It is a large digital database that houses information and pointers and guidelines for effective Internet usage. These include online community memberships, fundraising activities, history of organisations, aims of a campaign, contacts, and many more. The Internet can also be used for publication to advance a specific cause or agenda. Groups and individuals can use websites, blogs, and other social-networking sites such as Facebook to post events, send e-mails to newsgroups, and create posts. In this sense, social media serves as a platform to engage supporters and recruit potential supporters and other online audiences.

In addition, the Internet serves as a social space for both public and private dialogues on issues of concern, to debate or comment on the latest issues, to influence the actions of others, or to answer questions. Such interaction may assist in fostering new policy decisions and influencing public opinion. It is noticeable that *dialogic* messages (such as "I believe") on websites also attempt to foster a relationship amongst community members via *bonding* messages (such as "thank you") and *acknowledgement* postings (such as "noted"). Coordination of action is another way in which activists use the Internet. The Internet aids in the decision-making process by enabling individuals to post event details or distribute plans for mobilising the actions of the group and coordinate schedules. Users can make necessary arrangements without regard to the constraints of time and geography. Finally, the Internet is used for lobbying decision-makers by asking individuals to respond in support of a cause, whether it is to join a movement, post an image, e-mail the authorities, sign petitions, or even share their concerns to influence change.

Youth engage themselves online for various activities such as entertainment, socialisation, communication, and posting their opinions on current issues. They, however, engage less in discussing social issues online. There have been initiatives to increase civic engagement amongst youth. For example, in developed countries like the United States, TakingITGlobal.org is an organisation that works to overturn the perception that youth are apathetic about social issues; they simply lack access to appealing forms of engagement. The site was launched in 2000 with the intention of encouraging online engagement amongst youth. In its early iterations, the site had member and organisational profiles and discussion boards. Other tools, including blogs, an online art gallery, and online project planning tools followed. The site has evolved into a complex platform, tying together the core tools that youth use to participate via blogs, discussions boards, podcasts, and instant messaging, combined with collaborative action-planning tools and background information. The site supports learning, dialogue, collaboration, and action on key topics, including arts and media, culture and identity, human rights and equity, learning and education, environment and urbanisation, work and economics, health and wellness, peace, conflict, and governance, and technology and innovation.

Online Civic Engagement amongst Youth

The trends in youth civic engagement depend on the type of civic behaviour. Some argue that gratification influences the use of social media for entertainment, information-seeking, and social interaction. Dunne, Lawlor, and Rowley 2010; Raacke and Raacke 2008; Syvertsen, Wray-Lake, Flanagan, Briddell, and Osgood (2008), found that youth participation in "conventional" civic activities (participation in government, writing to a public official, etc.) has decreased over time. They found that participation in community service (activities that directly help others in the local community) has increased. From these results, we see that youth are increasingly active in directly helping others in their community but show decreased engagement with government and the political process in general.

Not surprisingly, trust in government amongst youth is also relatively low. A recent report by the Girl Scouts Research Institute (2009), surveying approximately three thousand teen boys and girls, found that civic engagement, including participation in political processes, giving to charity, and involvement in community service was up from twenty years previous. Although these studies do not specifically look at the impact of social media, they appear to illustrate that in the virtual area, youth civic engagement has risen. This, however, has excluded their involvement in government-related activities.

This chapter highlights the issues and challenges of using social media for online civic engagement amongst youths in Malaysia. These issues and challenges are important for the various stakeholders who are directly and indirectly affected in the development of youths' activities and programmes. In addition, the impact of social media on the influences of future generation-building for the country should be properly addressed, to ensure that we produce more responsible citizens. The next section describes the issues of social media for civic engagement amongst youths.

Issues on Online Civic Engagement amongst Youths

(a) Social Media as Communication Channel for Democracy and Justice

Social media can be used as a communication channel amongst citizens, including youths. This enhances the communication platform amongst citizens for many purposes. Civic scholars have examined predictors of online civic engagement in the context of political interest and political efficacy (Nam 2012) and sociodemographic markers (Boulianne 2009). In terms of age, Jensen, et al. (2007) found the younger generations were more apt to be e-citizens who utilise the social media platform for communication with government. There is evidence that social media have also been used by other citizens for addressing politics and government issues (Kumar and Vragov 2009; Baumgartner and Morris 2010). Examples of these movements are evident in Egypt for democracy and justice (Ali 2011; Choudhary, et al. 2012); for better reach, relevancy, and engagement in India (Rajapat 2009); on e-democracy in the United States (Nam 2011); and organising protests in Chile (Valenzuela, et al. 2012). Nonetheless, the usage of social media for promoting democracy and justice are not clearly shown in Malaysia, because these types of studies are scarce.

(b) Social Media for Bridging the Communication Gap between Government and Youth

Online civic-engagement efforts deploying social media are seen by the government as important tools for managing and delivering many of their strategic programmes to the citizens. These include the use of social media for managing national crisis situations (Kavanaugh, et al. 2012), for improving citizen-government communications (Jaeger et al. 2012), and for internal public-sector use as e-government initiatives (Bretschneider and Mergel 2010). Because it provides a open platform for discussions of and participation in national issues, social media can be an effective communication tool to bridge the gap between government and youth. With the provisions of a social-media platform, the lack of youth civic engagement on social issues could be reduced.

(c) Social Media for Managing Social Problems

Social media are often used as tools for managing social problems. Encounters from Brazil narrated by McCafferty (2011) studied the usage of social media for social interaction with high-profile leaders, for self-expression, and for political discussions. Labour unions have also deployed social media for their own causes (Bryson, et al. 2011; Zachary 2011). Social media has been applied as a natural social-marketing tool in support for curbing social problems, especially amongst youths. For example, the "fast unto death" campaign from seventy-two-year-old social activist Anna Hazare went viral, which brought thousands to the streets in support to fight against corruption (Visvanathan 2012). The same approach could further be applied in fighting against other social problems which are prominent amongst youths such as teen pregnancy, juvenile crimes, and decreasing moral values.

(d) Effective Usage of Social Media as a Social Marketing Tool

Some researchers suggest that social media are effective marketing tools that tailor to not only health awareness but environmental issues as well (Buis 2011; Liang and Scammon 2011; Ahmed, et al. 2010; Van de Belt, et al. 2012). Health awareness includes, for example, initiatives in combating the spread of HIV (Jaganath, et al. 2012). In Canada, Martinello and Donelle's (2012) qualitative study on the postings of a group of university students on Facebook underscored the students' use of this type of social media for environmental advocacy. In both situations, social media would be able to enhance the participation of youths in online discussions in promoting health and environment awareness.

(e) Lack of Civic Participation amongst Youth Citizens

While the decline in civic engagement over the past thirty years is evident amongst all age groups, it is particularly acute amongst the age of 18 to 29 (Delli Carpini 2000). Inclusive participation is a primary component of a civil society, yet opportunities and pathways for youthful civic engagement remain limited (Camino and Zeldin 2002). Youths have been criticised for their lack of involvement in social issues.

Challenges of Social Media for Civic Engagement

(a) The Challenge of Developing Social-Media Governance for Communication

In order to ensure that social media is used for democracy and justice, there is need for a policy to govern the usage of social media, not only amongst youths but all citizens in a country. A sound policy, meaning one that takes into consideration the potential impact on citizens' lives and community well-being, needs to be developed. Social-media governance has been identified as involving strategies, establishing guidelines for users, implementing monitoring tools, and offering training and a range of support to inform and guide social-media use (Fink and Zerfass 2010). A lack of any substantial governance framework leaves many organisations exposed to significant risks, as identified by Zerfass, Fink, and Linke (2010) and the Information Systems Audit and Control Association (ISACA 2011). In a study of social-media governance done in Australia, it was found that government departments and agencies are amongst the most enthusiastic adopters of social media, despite innate conservatism and traditionally restrictive policies in relation to staff making public comment (MacNamara 2011). As such, there is a need for our government to develop a policy on governing social-media usage for promoting democracy and justice.

(b) The Challenge of Social-Media Development as a Liaison Application with Authorities

A difficult but also essential matter will be for the government to articulate regulations with the companies and organisations that host the networked public sphere. These include Facebook, Twitter, Wikipedia, and YouTube (United States), QQ (China), WikiLeaks (a repository of leaked documents whose servers are in Sweden), Tuenti (Spain), and Naver (Korea). These are popular social-media sites used mostly for political speech, conversation, and coordination (Shirky 2011). If certain policies are regulated to control and monitor tracking of agreed content, such as pornography, racism, and terrorism, then some social problems may decrease. The next issue would then be on how to manage the issue of freedom of speech and content on the Internet.

(c) The Challenge of Developing Social-Media Strategy as an Alert System to Combat Social Problems

There are two arguments against the idea that social media will make a difference in addressing national social problems. The first is that the tools are themselves insufficient for actual civic actions. Secondly, there is a possibility that social media can produce as much harm to "democratisation as good, because repressive governments are becoming better at using these tools to suppress dissent" (Shirky 2011, 9). Some authors have critiqued the use of social media as an effective tool to mobilise civic actions, which has amounted to *slacktivism* (Gladwell 2010; Christensen 2011; Mengyang 2013), online actions that create a "feel-good" factor but have very limited real-life impact. An example of this includes clicking "Like" on Facebook – but doing nothing more. Protest movements – including democracy protests in Egypt (Choudhary 2012), beef protests in South Korea (CNN. com, 2008), and protests against education laws in Chile (Fábrega 2009) – have used social media as a coordinating platform for action. Unfortunately, these actions exposed participants to the threat of violence in the protests. In such cases, the message was sent across loudly to officials, but at no small cost to the safety of citizens and the country's reputation.

One way to develop a meaningful and productive social-media strategy in combating social issues is to by partnering with the public for problem-solving projects. The government, NGOs, and activists need to reach out to the people to get input, rather than blocking them out. There have been cases where public figures post speeches and videos on social media but disabled the function for comments and feedback, shutting down the Internet, or imposing censorship on civic expressions (see examples from Farthing 2010; Dunn 2011; King, et al. 2012). Rather, officials ought to be open to opinions and ideas which may foster civic participation online and further eradicate social problems. Some questions that we need to answer might include, "How could social-media sites be designed to better meet the needs of city officials?" and "What do officials envision as the challenges and opportunities for using social media to engage citizens?" The answers to the questions provide an opportunity for building social capital via public engagement.

(d) Application of Social Media as an Effective Marketing Tool for Civic Engagement

Imbuing social marketing with an existing civic (in particular, political) agenda has also proven to be challenging, running the risk of exacerbating cynicism about civic engagement amongst young people. For example, Australian Prime Minister John Howard used YouTube to publish a recorded reading of a media release. The comments function that would allow individuals to interact with the clip was turned off. This could be seen as the emergence of a form of "lip service to young people's political forms, rather than a genuine interest in engaging young people" (Farthing 2010, 186). In a more positive encounter, it was reported in the *American Journal of Transplantation* that Facebook helped boost the number of people who registered themselves as organ donors in a single day by a twenty-one fold (Castillo 2013). The challenge is to have social media seen as a positive tool in marketing civic involvement to the public.

(e) The Need to Increase Youth Involvement in Addressing Social Problems

It has been implied that no other group is as disengaged from civic engagements as youth. These anxieties have been echoed globally.

Academics and public figures often claim that young people are politically apathetic and lack civic awareness (Delli Capini 2000, Bessant 2004, Bennet 2008). For instance, voter turnout in the United States trails that of other industrialised societies, and is particularly anaemic amongst voters between the ages of eighteen and twenty-four (Iyengar and Jackman 2004). In the United Kingdom, there was an alarmingly low turnout of the aforementioned age group in the 2001 and 2005 general elections (Sloam 2007). On Australia Day in 2005, Australia's governor-general presented the concerns about the issue on young Australians deserting civic engagement:

> There is a worrying trend of disengagement from our democratic process particularly amongst younger Australians. The issues that interest them are often overshadowed by the rough and tumble of politics, however justified that may be in a robust democracy. If we cannot find ways to spark their interest and involvement, we risk the consequences of more young Australians simply turning away. (Jeffery 2005)

In response to these concerns, many have urged experts to look into the different approaches, including the use of the Internet or new technologies, to draw young people in civic matters. For example, on page 21 of *Changing Citizenship in the Digital Age,* editor W. Lance Bennett argues that the public needs to "bridge the paradigms" or else youth, digitally inspired or not, will continue to get disconnected from formal civic life. He argues in favour of a better approach, such as showing young people how, through their use of new technologies and otherwise, they can have an impact on the political process. In another instance, Raynes-Goldie and Luke Walker (2008) took a deep dive into youth participation in the civic engagement site known as

TakingITGlobal. Their findings point to online civic-engagement sites as primarily facilitators of action, a promising hope for youth to be civically aware and engaged. In such instances, the challenge is to attract youth using social media for civic actions in real life.

References

Ahmed, O H, et al. (2010). "iSupport: Do Social Networking Sites Have a Role to Play in Concussion Awareness?" *Disability and Rehabilitation*, 32(22), 1877–1883. doi: 10.3109/09638281003734409.

Ali, A (2011). "The Power of Social Media in Developing Nations". *Human Rights Journal*, 24(1), 185–219.

Avery, E, et al. (2010). "Diffusion of Social Media Among Public Relations Practitioners in Health Departments Across Various Community Population Sizes". *Journal of Public Relations Research*, 22(3), 336-358. doi: 10.1080/10627261003614427.

Baumgartner, J C, and J S Morris (2010). "MyFaceTube Politics: Social Networking Web Sites and Political Engagement of Young Adults". *Social Science Computer Review*, 28(1), 24–44.

Bessant, J (2004). "Mixed Messages: Youth Participation and Democratic Practice". *Australian Journal of Political Science*, 39(2), 387–404.

Boulianne, S (2009). "Does Internet Use Affect Engagement? A Meta-Analysis of Research". *Political Communication*, 26(2), 193–211.

Bretschneider, S I, and I Mergel (2010). "Technology and Public Management Information Systems: Where Have We Been and Where Are We Going". *The State of Public Administration: Issues, Problems and Challenges*, 187–203.

Bryson, A, Gomez, R, and P Willman (2010). "Online Social Networking and Trade Union Membership: What the Facebook |Phenomenon Truly Means for Labor Organisers". *Labor History*, 51(1), 41–53. doi: 10.1080/00236561003654719.

Buis, L R (2011). "The Potential for Web-Based Social Network Sites and Self-Regulation for Health Promotion". *American Journal of Health Promotion*, 26(2), 73–76.

Camino, L, and S Zeldin (2002). "From Periphery to Center: Pathways for Youth Civic Engagement in the Day-to-Day Life of Communities". *Applied Developmental Science,* 6(4), 213–220.

Castillo, M (2013). "Study: Allowing Organ Donation Status on Facebook Increased Number of Donors". Retrieved 5 August 2013 from *http://www.cbsnews.com/8301–204_162–57589833/study-allowing-organ-donation-status-on-facebook-increased-number-of-donors/.*

Choudhary, A, et al. (2012). "Social Media Evolution of the Egyptian Revolution". *Communications of the ACM,* 55(5), 74–80. doi: 10.1145/2160718.2160736.

Christensen, H S (2011). "Political Activities on the Internet: Slacktivism or Political Participation by Other Means?" *First Monday,* 16(2).

CNN.com (2008). "Scores Hurt in S. Korea Beef Protests". Retrieved 5 March 2013, from *http://edition.cnn.com/2008/WORLD/asiapcf/06/29/skorea.beef/.*

Delli Carpini, M X (2000). "Gen.com: Youth, Civic Engagement, and the New Information Environment". *Political Communication,* 17(4), 341–349.

Dunn, A (2011). "Unplugging a Nation: State Media Strategy During Egypt's January 25 Uprising". *Fletcher F. World Aff.,* 35, 15.

Denning, Dorothy (2000). "Activism, Hacktivism, and Cyberterrorism: The Internet as a Tool for Influencing Foreign Policy". *The Computer Security Journal,* XVI (Summer), 15–35.

Department of Statistic, M (2009). "Social Trends in Malaysia." Retrieved 12 March 2012 from *http://www.statistics.gov.my/portal/download_Labour/files/BPTMS/PST-Siri11.pdf.*

Dunne, Á, Lawlor, M-A, and J Rowley (2010). "Young People's Use of Online Social Networking Sites – A Uses and Gratifications Perspective". *Journal of Research in Interactive Marketing,* 4(1),46–58.

Fábrega, J (2009). "Education: Three Years After Chile's Penguin Revolution". Retrieved 17 April 2013 from *http://www.americasquarterly.org/node/982.*

Farthing, R (2010). "The Politics of Youthful Antipolitics: Representing the 'Issue' of Youth Participation in Politics". *Journal of Youth Studies,* 13(2), 181–195.

Facebook (2010). Statistics. Retrieved from *http://www.facebook.com/press/info.php?statistics.*

Facebook (2012). "What Is Tagging and How Does it Work?" Retrieved 1 October 2012 from *http://www.facebook.com/help/124970597582337/.*

Fink, S, and A Zerfass (2010). "Social Media Governance 2010: How Companies, the Public Sector, and NGOs Handle the Challenge of Transparent Communication on the Internet". Research report. Liepzig, Germany: University of Leipzig and Fink and Fuchs PR. Retrieved from *http://www.ffpr.de/fileadmin/user_upload/PDF-Dokumente/Social_Media_Governance_2010_-_Results-final.pdf.*

Gil de Zúñiga, H and S Valenzuela (2011). "The Mediating Path to a Stronger Citizenship: Online and Offline Networks, Weak Ties, and Civic Engagement." *Communication Research* 38(3): 397–421.

Girl Scout Research Institute. (2009). "Good Intentions: The Belief and Values of Teens and Twins Today". Retrieved 28 August 2010 from *http://*www.*girlscouts.org/.*

Gladwell, M (2010). "Small Change – Why the Revolution Will Not Be Tweet". Retrieved 3 March 2012 from *http://www.newyorker.com/reporting/2010/10/04/101004fa_fact_gladwell?currentPage=all.*

ISACA (Information Systems Audit and Control Association) (2011). "Social Media: Business Benefits and Security, Governance and Assurance Perspectives". White Paper. Retrieved from *http://www.isaca.org/Knowledge-Center/Research/Pages/White-Papers.aspx.*

Iyengar, S and S Jackman (2004). *Technology and Politics: Incentives for Youth Participation* (Vol. 24): CIRCLE.

Jaganath, D., H K Gill, et al. (2012). "Harnessing Online Peer Education (HOPE): Integrating C-POL and Social Media to Train Peer Leaders in HIV Prevention." *AIDS Care* 24(5): 593–600.

Kumar, N and R Vragov (2009). "Active Citizen Participation Using ICT Tools". *Communications of the ACM,* 52(1), 118–121.

Kavanaugh, A L, et al. (2012). "Social Media Use by Government: From the Routine to the Critical". *Government Information Quarterly,* 29(4), 480–491. doi: http://dx.doi.org/10.1016/j.giq.2012.06.002.

Jeffery, M (2005). Australia Day address 2005. Retrieved 1 November 2009 from *http://www.gg.gov.au/governorgeneral/speech.php?id=324.*

King, G, Pan, J, and M Roberts (2012). *How Censorship in China Allows Government Criticism but Silences Collective Expression.* Paper presented at the APSA 2012 Annual Meeting.

Liang, B, and D L Scammon (2011). "E-Word-of-Mouth on Health Social Networking Sites: An Opportunity for Tailored Health Communication". *Journal of Consumer Behaviour,* 10(6),322–331. doi: 10.1002/cb.378.

Martinello, N and L Donelle (2012). "Online Conversations among Ontario University Students: Environmental Concerns." *Informatics for Health and Social Care* 37(3): 177–189.

Montgomery, K, Gottlieb-Robles, B, and G O Larson (2004). "Youth as e-Citizens: Engaging the Digital Generation". Washington, DC: Center for Social Media, School of Communication, American University. Retrieved 26 February 2011 from *http://www.centerforsocialmedia.org/ecitizens/youthreport.pdf.*

MacNamara, J (2011). "Social Media Strategy and Governance: Gaps, Risks and Opportunities". Australian Centre for Public Communication, University of Technology, Sydney.

McCafferty, D (2011). "Brave, New Social World". *Communications of the ACM,* 54(7), 19–21.

Mengyang, Z Z (2013). *Gauging Slacktivism in China: Taking Microblog Users as an Example.* The Chinese University of Hong Kong.

Nam, T (2011). "Whose e-Democracy? The Democratic Divide in American Electoral Campaigns". *Information Polity: The International Journal of Government and Democracy in the Information Age,* 16(2), 131–150. doi: 10.3233/ip-2011-0220.

Pasek, J, et al. (2006). "America's Youth and Community Engagement – How Use of Mass Media Is Related to Civic Activity and Political Awareness in 14-to 22-Year-Olds". *Communication Research,* 33(3), 115–135.

The Performance Management and Delivery Unit (PEMANDU) Lab Highlights on Crime Report (2009). Retrieved from *www.pemandu.gov.my.*

Putnam, R D (2000). *Bowling Alone: The Collapse and Revival of American Community.* New York: Simon and Schuster.

Raacke, J and J Bonds-Raacke (2008). "MySpace and Facebook: Applying the Uses and Gratifications Theory to Exploring Friend-Networking Sites". *CyberPsychology and Behavior,* 11(2), 169–174. doi: 10.1089/cpb.2007.0056.

Rajapat, V (2009). "Social Media: Trends and Growth of Digital Media". *Siliconindia,* 12(6), 28–30.

Ramakrishnan, S Karthick and Mark Baldassare (2004). *The Ties That Bind: Changing Demographics and Civic Engagement in California.* San Francisco, Calif.: Public Policy Institute of California.

Raynes-Goldie, K and L Walker (2008). "Our Space: Online Civic Engagement Tools for Youth". *Civic Life Online: Learning How Digital Media Can Engage Youth.* Edited by W. Lance Bennett. The John D. and Catherine T. MacArthur Foundation Series on Digital Media And Learning. Cambridge, Mass.: The MIT Press.

Shirky, C (2011). "Political Power of Social Media – Technology, the Public Sphere, and Political Change". *Foreign Aff.,* 90, 28.

Sloam, J (2007). "Rebooting Democracy: Youth Participation in Politics in the UK". *Parliamentary Affairs,* 60(4), 548–567.

_____. 2008. "Teaching Democracy: The Role of Political Science Education". *British Journal of Politics and International Relations* 10(3): 509–24.

Syvertsen, A K, et al. (2008). Network on Transitions to Adulthood Research Network.

Verba, S, Schlozman, K, and B Henry (1995). *Voice and Equality: Civic Voluntarism in American Politics.* Cambridge, Mass.: Harvard University Press.

Visvanathan, S (2012). "Anna Hazare and the Battle Against Corruption". *Cultural Critique* (81), 103–111.

Weissberg, R (2005). *The Limits of Civic Activism: Cautionary Tales on the Use of Politics.* New Brunswick, NJ: Transaction Publishers.

Zachary, M-K (2011). "Social-Networking Sites in a Union Setting – Part 1". *Supervision,* 72(2), 20–23.

Zhang, W, Johnson, T J, Seltzer, T, and S L Bichard (2010). "The Revolution Will Be Networked the Influence of Social-Networking Sites on Political Attitudes and Behavior". *Social Science Computer Review,* 28(1), 75–92. doi: 10.1177/0894439309335162.

CHAPTER FIVE

Social Media for Social Advances: Use of Social Media in Educating Future Generations

Farrah Dina Yusop,[1] Rafiza Abd Razak,[1] and Siti Mariam Muhammad Abd Basar[2]

Summary: This chapter will focus on discussion of two educational issues and four challenges related to successful technology integration into the Malaysian school system. The two issues are the teaching-to-the-test approach, widely adopted by Malaysian teachers, and the generational gaps between teachers and students. These two issues include four main challenges that impede the educational-technology movement in Malaysia, specifically a lack of facilities and infrastructure to support technology implmentation, a lack of on-site technology support, a lack of time to plan and implement technology-based instructions, and a heavy teacher workload. Social media, with its cost-effective and easy-to-use features, is highlighted as providing promising educational tools ready to be used in instructional improvement.

[1] Department of Curriculum and Instructional Technology, Faculty of Education, University of Malaya, 50603 Kuala Lumpur, Malaysia.
[2] Faculty of Education, University of Malaya, 50603 Kuala Lumpur, Malaysia.

The authors also discuss how social media could be used to support four aspects of education, specifically communication, collaboration, presentation, and edutainment. Further research on social media is recommended to further understanding of its functionality as an educational tool.

Introduction

Based on both the current and predicted needs of society, our current educational system has undergone continuous modification and reform. What makes it necessary to launch these modifications and reforms now? While many scholars have proposed their own theories with respect to understanding the current problems with our education system, this chapter focuses on only two main issues: the teaching-to-the-test instructional approach as a response to the current exam-oriented educational system and generational differences amongst teachers/educators and learners.

Teaching-to-the-Test Instructional Approaches

Educational scholars agree that any assessment based on an individual student's whole-self performance is a superior and fair approach to evaluating one's educational achievements. In this context, *whole-self performance* refers to a student's intellectual, emotional, physical, social, aesthetic, and spiritual development. This is also referred to as an *holistic educational approach* (Miller 2007). This approach proposes that schools need to be a place for nurturing and enhancing student joy, wholeness, and sense-of-life purposes, rather than just focusing solely on cognitive abilities.

Our current educational system, in its own unique way, favours those with excellent academic achievements, despite the introduction of many curriculum modifications and system reforms. Since academic performance is still being used as the sole metric with which to measure a student's success, curricula tend to be designed for and heavily focused on preparing students for various standardised tests. In such an environment, teachers tend to be more comfortable in adopting *the teaching-to-the-test* approach, an approach that favours rote memorisation rather than an evaluation of critical and creative thinking skills. Students are being told that they need pay attention to only specific correct answers to questions, which tends to cause them to become only passive recipients of knowledge.

Generational Gap

The issue of the generational gap between teachers and students has been discussed and debated only in a limited way in the educational literature. It has, however, been a popular topic of conversation in the business world. Much corporate training now focuses on understanding the unique *behaviours* by which different generations perceive, act, learn, and work, so that appropriate training can be delivered.

There are at least four categories of generations identified in the literature. They are the baby boomers (born after 1945), Generation X (born between 1961 and 1981), Generation Y/the millennials (born between 1982 and 2000), and Gen Z (born after 2000). Generations Y and Z, when compared to the majority of baby boomers and Generation Xers, tend to be more technology-savvy groups who utilise technology to complete daily tasks. They also tend to be socially connected with their family, friends, co-workers, and many other social groups via their technological devices, rather than by the personal, face-to-face communication mechanisms favoured by earlier generations.

With an understanding of the unique characteristics of these groups, it is interesting to consider generational gaps between them and their impact on teaching and learning. Our schools are flooded by the younger generations (Y and Z), while the majority of the teachers are either baby boomers or members of Generations X and Y. Technology-wise, baby-boomer teachers may be slow in trying to keep up with current technologies, while generation X and Y teachers, while they may already be technology users, are still finding it a struggle to integrate technology into their daily instructional tasks, due to the technical, systemic, and individual challenges they face Their attitudes and preferences towards technology may therefore be very different from those of younger generations, and this may profoundly impact the way they teach. Because of their relatively limited technological knowledge and skills (as compared to those of their students), they may be more likely to favour the talk-and-chalk approach. They also may emphasise a teacher-centred rather than learner-centred approach that fits well with their own personal attitudes and the current school environment.

These two educational issues have affected the way many schools operate. Technology has been applauded as the solution to many educational problems, but after years of implementing technologies in school contexts, no significant changes on students' academic performances have been observed.

Challenges in Implementing Technology in the Malaysian Educational System

Technology implementation in Malaysian schools has gone through several changes in every decade, and many initiatives have been undertaken to rectify problems in technology implementation. Nonetheless, the rapid changes in the development of technological applications in education demands that educators have the ability to stay informed with trends in the field and to respond quickly to evolving student needs. But are teachers well equipped with competent skills to face technological change? With respect to educational-technology implementation in schools, the following are deemed to be the main challenges currently surrounding the Malaysian educational system

Challenge 1: Facility Limitations

One of the biggest limitations in implementing technology in the process of teaching and learning is limited access to adequate and high-quality facilities in the school setting. Research has indicated that ideally, access would translate to one-to-one computing (Chuang, Thompson, and Schmidt 2003; Pamuk and Thompson 2009), meaning one student per Internet-connected computer. Most schools, however, have been unable to realise this situation due to the high cost of providing such access.

Malaysian classrooms are overcrowded with students. A typical Malaysian classroom serves thirty to forty students. If the government was to provide each student with technological access, the associated costs would be tremendous. The only workable solution is to provide one computer lab equipped with one teacher desktop and up to thirty student computers with Internet access and a shared printer. This solution, however, results in three educational challenges.

First, the teaching and learning processes have to be conducted in the computer lab. This means that the teacher may have to physically move the whole classroom of thirty to forty students to this lab from another room or another building. The time involved in this movement from one place to another consumes minutes better allocated to teaching the subject. Each block of teaching typically consists of a thirty- to forty-minute time slot. If students took ten minutes to walk to the lab and another ten minutes to walk back to the classroom, then twenty minutes of classroom instruction is wasted on just walking back and forth.

Second, most computer labs are physically locked and use keypads for safety and security reasons. A teacher would need to first get permission to use the lab from the lab coordinator and subsequently get the lab key from the school administration office. Because only one or two computer labs are typically available to cater to the needs of the entire school, teachers need to take turns in using them. This means that they must plan the use of a computer lab far in advance.

Moreover, the time slot available may not be compatible with the intended lesson plan, so teachers might need to readjust their instructional plans. The whole process of getting permission, waiting for their turns, and later adjusting lesson plans to the available time slots can easily frustrate teachers and might result in their resistance to using technology at all.

Challenge 2: Lack of Technological Support

Access to technology alone does not guarantee its effective utilisation. Many schools are equipped with the latest computers; some provide the best Internet connections but are lacking real-life technical consultants able to provide on-site technical help when needed. This situation leaves teachers with no other choice but to ignore using computers for teaching and revert to a more feasible option of not using technology at all.

Each school needs to have an on-site technical team available during school hours for troubleshooting, maintenance, and continuous support. In many developed countries, on-site technological-support teams have proven to be helpful and strengthen/facilitate technology-implementation efforts. Having such a team available will give teachers peace of mind, as they can focus on their teaching instead of worrying about technical issues.

Challenge 3: Lack of Time to Plan and Implement Technology-Based Instruction

Technology-based instruction requires a tremendous amount of time on a teacher's part to plan and implement. The biggest issue is that technology-based teaching and learning activities must be aligned with the pre-identified national curriculum. The Malaysian educational system is a centralised system in which all curriculum processes (such as planning and designing) are determined by the Ministry of Education. In this situation, teachers play a relatively passive role as curriculum implementers with little or no power to modify the prescribed curriculum.

This situation invites another issue, that of finding suitable materials and readily available specific resources for teaching the curriculum. Most online materials are in English; the curriculum is taught in the local language. This means that most of the time, teachers must design their own materials suitable for their students' cognitive levels. Such activity is time-consuming, given the fact that teachers have other non-teaching tasks to be completed within the allotted time.

Moreover, each subject-matter component has its own prescribed time limit of forty-five minutes per class session. If a teacher consumes the first five minutes to set up the computer lab or to align the laptops with class projectors and another final five minutes to shut down the computers and reset the projectors, the teacher would be left with only thirty-five minutes solely for instruction. Within this thirty-five-minute time interval, teachers also need to perform classroom-management activity such as marking students' attendance, attending to all thirty to forty individual students' characters, and troubleshooting computers. They thus may be left with only a few minutes to complete their instruction. Ultimately, they may easily become frustrated and opt not to implement any technology-based instruction at all.

Challenge 4: Heavy Teacher Workload

Teaching is a socially related profession because education is of interest to all members of society. Educational institutions are always under constant pressure to revamp their curricula and teaching approaches, in order to remain current with the current and future needs of the society. Consequently, the teaching profession is always under scrutiny, and teachers are continuously asked to keep up with recent technological trends. Since student failure is often connected with teaching failure, teaching is one of the most stressful professions, and teachers are leaving the profession at an alarming rate (Fisher 2011).

One of the biggest factors contributing to teacher stress is heavy workload. Teachers are often responsible not only for teaching-related tasks but also for administrative tasks. In Malaysia, it is common for teachers to record classroom attendance, record incidents of student misbehaviour, accompany students to sports and other social events, collect academic and non-academic fees, and bring students to clinics or hospitals in cases of unexpected illness during school hours, to mention just a few tasks. These non-teaching tasks always distract teachers from focussing on improving the quality of their own instruction.

Ironically, each curriculum modification and reform initiative intended to enhance teaching and learning has usually ended with more and more administrative work being imposed upon teachers, until the number of administrative tasks required of teachers actually exceeds the number of teaching-related tasks.

The Way Forward

So far, this chapter has discussed several challenges in implementing educational technology in the Malaysian school system. They include facility limitations, lack of on-site technology support, lack of time for planning and implementing technology-based instruction, and heavy teacher workload. Some of these challenges appear identical to those in other countries, especially in the United Kingdom and the United States; some are specific to the Malaysian setting only.

Can we find practical solutions to address these challenges? The next section of this chapter presents a snapshot of a current Malaysian educational-technology initiative for enabling technology-based teaching and learning in schools. It also proposes utilisation of various online media, including social media, as practical and cost-effective alternatives to the massively customised technologies often adopted today in efforts to elevate the quality of the Malaysian educational system.

National Educational Technology Plan

Realising these challenges in the Malaysian educational system, a new technological initiative called 1BestariNet was launched in 2010 to provide schools with more computers, together with high-capacity wireless Internet access to support technology-based teaching and learning approaches.

An online learning-management system called Frog Virtual Learning Environment (Frog-VLE) has been established as a Web-based learning platform intended to expand the learning experiences beyond the confined classroom setting. The platform is designated not only for teachers and students, but also for parents to use in tracking their children's learning progress.

Online Professional Development Courses for Teachers

Student learning and success are due in large part to the effectiveness of teachers. However, teaching workloads and time constraints often hinder teachers from spending adequate time in activities such as planning, preparing resources, observing colleagues' lessons, and continued professional development (CPD) (Deakin, et al. 2010).

Online CPD (or e-CPD) is a tremendously useful and applicable method used for enhancing teacher performance. Its online nature supports broad access to activities and learning resources. Teachers are able to discuss, collaborate, and share tasks or teaching resources with their online colleagues to plan and improve their teaching preparation and instructional activities.

While e-CPD seems to be an ideal solution to current face-to-face CPD, it must be carefully designed and closely monitored by e-CPD administrators and/or organisers. Reflecting on their own e-CPD experience with several groups of Malaysian in-service teachers, Rafiza, Farrah Dina, and Shahril Nizam (2013) concluded that e-CPD could be a complete failure without the continuous participation, collaboration, and technical support between administrators and teachers. They also mention that sustaining teacher motivation to actively participate in the online environment has proven to be a great challenge. Amongst other factors, they associate the challenge of teacher comfort while interacting in an online environment. If teachers feel uncomfortable interacting online, they would not participate actively in discussions and vice versa. They recommend that teachers be exposed to an e-training environment prior to the e-CPD session and be equipped with necessary technical skills to interact, so as to boost the level of their confidence in using the technology. Their views are somewhat similar to those of Snoeyink and Ertmer (2002), who stated that the negative elements – limited resources, lack of time, lack of technical support, technical problems, teachers' lack of confidence, resistance to change, and negative attitudes with no perception of benefits – may slowly diminish as more effective training and administrative support is applied.

Utilisation of Social Media

Advancement of technology offers various possibilities in the form of technological tools, resources, and knowledge offerings. Because it is cost-effective and available to most students at no charge, social media is a potential technological tool that reduces or even eliminates financial challenges. The crux of social media is communication- and information-sharing, making it a great tool to be adapted for learning. Other features such as file-sharing, collaboration, and networking allow users to reside in a community where they can share and connect with other members.

Educators can take advantage of the opportunity to explore the variety of social-media tools offered and adapt them for use to accommodate their teaching needs and enhance the students' learning experiences. Social media can be used for many purposes, depending on educator experiences and creativity. This chapter will discuss the five most popular uses of social media in education.

Social Media for Communication Purposes

One popular social networking site, Facebook, can be utilised by teachers to support communication amongst their learners. Although the original purpose of Facebook was not educational, it can be adapted and used to support classroom instruction. Facebook allows interactive opportunities and sharing of files, videos, or links. Users can communicate with each other via messages, status updates, or commenting features. These features can also be used to present class ideas or online forum discussions related to their courses. In short, Facebook can be used for educators to connect with their students, especially outside of the classroom hours.

Social Media for Collaborative Writing Purposes

Wiki, an asynchronous and simple Web-based tool, has the potential to provide rich collaborating experiences amongst learners, whether inside or outside the classroom. The term "wiki" originated from the Hawaiian term *wiki wiki* which means "to hurry", implying that wikis enable rapid and easy authoring directly to the Web (Wheeler, Yeomans, and Wheeler 2008). Wiki enables a user to create a wiki page and to add, edit, or delete any content in his or her existing wiki. The commenting feature in Wiki allows students and teacher to interact with each other. Using Wiki, learners and teachers can communicate to share information and documents and work together in a virtual environment, regardless of geographic location. This makes Wiki a good tool for collaborative learning in which students learn and work together, instead of individually performing tasks. One example of using Wiki is collaborative writing exercises in which students can work together on a Wiki page by adding or editing pages written by their friends to accomplish the given writing task.

Social Media for Presentation Purposes

Presentations encourage visualisation, a valuable and interesting approach to expressing ideas and messages. Social-media presentation tools allow users to share their presentation slides online via the Web or cloud, to be shared with others.

Prezi is an example of a popular tool. It is an interactive online presentation tool that can be used to enhance creative thinking and get students engaged in a lesson. Prezi allows a user to use a storyboard approach to prepare a linear storyline for interesting presentations. The flexibility of Prezi allows users to present their ideas in many ways. Apart from that, Prezi's interactive presentation characteristics, such as its zooming feature, for example, enables teachers to create fun and creative notes or lectures, which in turn makes the lesson more fun and engaging than if more common software such as Microsoft PowerPoint was used.

Social Media for Edutainment Purposes

Social media can also be used for edutainment, in which games can be played via gaming websites or social networks. Users can choose whether to play individually or with their friends, which can encourage collaboration. Online games are popular amongst youngsters, so they can be integrated into educational approaches to motivate and increase student interest in learning. They also can be played through a wide variety of devices such as desktops, laptops, tablets, or video consoles with Internet connections.

Online games are popular, especially in language-learning classes, since they not only provide enjoyment and stimulation to learners, they also can encourage use of language in a creative and communicative manner. FunBrain.com is an example of an online gaming site that can be used for educational purposes. This website provides learning on topics like mathematics and reading. Classic board games, like Monopoly, are also available for users to play with friends or other users online. Monopoly contains elements of mathematics like counting.

In addition to Monopoly, Scrabble, the popular word and vocabulary game, can now be played online.

Conclusion

This chapter has focused on the teaching-to-the-test approach practiced by Malaysian schoolteachers and the generational gap between teachers and young learners as the two main educational issues confronting the current Malaysian educational system. It further lists four main challenges that impede successful technology integration, namely facility limitations, lack of on-site technology support, lack of time to plan and implement technology-based instruction, and heavy teacher workload.

While it recognises that issues and challenges will continue to affect effective technology integration, this chapter proposes the use of social media as a new and promising alternative technology, offering potential solutions to these challenges. Apart from its negligible costs, its simple and user-friendly nature allow users to easily use it in their daily routines. Social media could be used for purposes of communication, collaboration, presentation, and edutainment. Teachers and students could mix and match all of these exciting tools to suit their needs and achieve better learning attention amongst students. Although most of these tools have not been specifically developed for classroom purposes, creative teachers can always adapt them to transform learning into the fun-filled and intellectually stimulating activities our younger generations crave. More research on effective use of social media for teaching and learning purposes should be crafted and shared with academic practitioners so that our younger generations can be prepared to face the new technologically challenging world.

References

Bender, E (2004). "Rules of the Collaboratory Game". *MIT Technology Review.* Retrieved July 31ˢᵗ, 2013 from *http://www.technologyreview. com/news/403384/rules-of-the-collaboratory-game.*

Chuang, H H, Thompson, A, and D Schmidt (2003). "Faculty Technology Mentoring Programmes: Major Trends in the Literature". *Journal of Computing in Teacher Education,* 19(4), 101–106.

Deakin, G, James, N, Tickner, M, and J Tidswell (2010). "Teachers' Workload Diary Survey 2010", (DFE-RR057). UK Department of Education. Retrieved from *http://dera.ioe.ac.uk/11571/1/DFE-RR057-WEB.pdf.*

Fisher, M H (2011)."Factors Influencing Stress, Burnout, and Retention of Secondary Teachers". *Current Issues in Education,* 14(1), 37. Retrieved May 20ᵗʰ, 2014 from *http://cie.asu.edu/.*

Miller, J P (2007). *The Holistic Curriculum.* Toronto: University of Toronto Press.

Pamuk, S, and A D Thompson (2009). "Development of a Technology Mentor Survey Instrument: Understanding Student Mentors' Benefits". *Computers and Education,* 53(1), 14–23.

Rafiza, A R, Farrah Dina, Y, and S Shahril Nizam (2013). "Implementation of e-Continued Professional Development (E-CPD): Issues and Challenges". Paper presented at the International Conference on Creative Education, Singapore.

Snoeyink, R, and P A Ertmer (2002). "Thrust into Technology: How Veteran Teachers Respond". *Journal of Educational Technology Systems,* 30(1), 85–111.

Wheeler, S, Yeomans, P, and D Wheeler (2008). "The Good, the Bad, and the Wiki: Evaluating Student-Generated Content for Collaborative Learning". *British Journal of Educational Technology,* 39(6), 987–995.

CHAPTER SIX

Impression Management: Managing Followers' Impressions about Leaders' Effectiveness through Social Media

Sharmila Jayasingam,[1] **Sharan Kaur,**[1]
and Mahfooz A. Ansari[2]

Summary: Our goal in this chapter is to establish a link between social media and the impression management techniques used by leaders. While doing so, we will identify several issues and challenges associated with this link. The chapter has been organised into four sections. Section one is devoted to a brief overview on what impression management entails and some commonly identified tactics; this section is extended to discuss the use of social media for impression management. Section two explores the new partnership between leaders and social media. Section three explores the issues and challenges for leaders who employ social media to impression-manage. Section four surmises the future direction for the association between leaders and social media.

---

[1] Department of Business Policy and Strategy, Faculty of Business and Accountancy, University of Malaya, 50603 Kuala Lumpur, Malaysia.
[2] Faculty of Management, University of Lethbridge, Lethbridge, Canada.

Impression Management: An Overview

Impression management refers to the process by which an individual tries to manage perceptions formed about him or her (Leary and Kowalski 1990). Although people in general try to manage other people's impression about them without any conscious effort to create a specific impression, there may be cases in which individuals become driven to influence how others see them (Leary and Kowalski 1990).

One factor that drives individuals to impression-manage is when the impression they make facilitates goal accomplishment (Leary and Kowalski 1990). This factor gains additional prominence when the individual's behaviour is said to receive much publicity (Leary and Kowalski 1990). In addition, if the targets play a crucial role in conferring desired outcomes to those who impress them positively, the need to impression-manage increases tremendously (Leary and Kowalski 1990).

There are numerous taxonomies on impression-management tactics. The 1982 Jones and Pittman model has remained the most popular taxonomy that has been adopted or adapted in studies on impression management. This taxonomy outlined five impression-management tactics: self-promotion, exemplification, ingratiation, intimidation, and supplication. *Self-promotion* refers to attempts by individuals to appear more competent through the promotion of one's ability and accomplishment (Bolino and Turney 2003). *Exemplification* reflects the portrayal of exemplary individual effort that goes beyond the call of duty (Bolino and Turney 2003). *Ingratiation* involves attempts to flatter others or doing favours for others with hopes of being seen as likeable (Bolino and Turney 2003). On the contrary, *intimidation* involves an individual's attempt to appear intimidating by acting in a threatening manner (Bolino and Turney 2003). Finally, *supplication* entails broadcasting one's inadequacy in an attempt to be perceived as needy (Bolino and Turney 2003).

While these tactics remain widely used in most organisational and behavioural studies, the tactics may no longer be suitable for explaining individual impression management through social-media sites. The next section reviews impression management in social-media sites in general and highlights some emerging tactics that may be more popular in social media.

Social Media and Impression Management

The term *social media* refers to a group of websites where members can create, edit, and view what is called user-generated content (UGC). There are three types of social media based on the form: text-based, visual-orientated, and three-dimensional virtual-reality websites. *Text-based websites* involve blogs and collaborative projects such as Wikipedia. *Visual-orientated websites* include Facebook, Flickr, and YouTube that emphasise photo and video forms. Finally, *three-dimensional websites* encompass virtual social worlds such as Second Life (Kaplan and Haenlein 2010).

Social-media platforms can be further categorised into seven common types based on purpose. This categorization includes *social networks* (e.g., Facebook, LinkedIn, MySpace), *book-marking sites* (e.g., Delicious, StumbledUpon, Dropbox), *social news* (e.g., Digg, Reddit), *media-sharing* (e.g., YouTube, Flickr), *microblogging* (e.g., Twitter), *blogs and forums*, and *employee-ideation programmes*. Some platforms, such as social networks, exist to connect people with similar interests and backgrounds. Other sites (e.g., bookmarking sites, social news, media sharing, and so forth) allow the sharing of links, media, updates, and other relevant information. Fundamentally, connectivity is the key characteristic which defines social media, regardless of its form or role.

Social media has been used extensively in managing impression. Social media such as Facebook and Twitter facilitate the carving of individuality of a brand, especially when the person in-charge manages the postings personally (Deiser and Newton 2013). In view of social media's role in impression management, organisations are employing more than one social-media website simultaneously (Jantos and Brulhart 2010; Johnston 2010). AirAsia, for example, aside from drawing Internet users to its official website, employs Blogger, Facebook, Flickr, Twitter, and YouTube (AirAsia 2011). On Facebook, members could show their support by clicking a "like" button. Malaysian companies, such as AirAsia, amassed a total of 2,561,498 "likes" till to-date (July 2014). Other popular Malaysian companies on Facebook are Secret Recipe with 315,012 "Likes" and Old Town White Coffee with 65,676 "Likes" (July 2014). Similarly, individuals engage in activities such as status updates, uploading photos, commenting, and "liking" friends' post in an attempt to manage people's impression about them and appear likeable (Wong 2012).

While some individuals or organisations still rely on the common impression-management tactics identified by Jones and Pittman (1982), some studies have highlighted a shift in impression-management tactics employed through social media. For example, Chen (2009) claims that impression management via social-media sites such as YouTube no longer relies on the traditional impression management tactics delineated by Jones and Pittman (1982). On the contrary, additional emerging tactics such as *basking* (enhancement of image by asserting connection with important others) and *mystery* (maintaining a mystifying identity in order to accentuate their talent and not draw attention to their physical appearance) are being employed to manage impressions through YouTube. Fundamentally, in addition to the commonly used tactics, organisations also use social media to impression-manage through various strategies such as communication with consumers, target advertisements, and spreading awareness through the word of mouth.

First, companies communicate with social-media members and gain recruits, product awareness, brand loyalty, as well as conduct free research (Johnston 2010; Kitchen 1999; Pavlik 2007). For example, British Airways posted a video on YouTube as part of their pilot-recruitment drive (McNeill 2011). Companies such as Nike and Disney engage in social media to interact with the public and gain consumer feedback (Constantinides and Fountain 2008). Businesses use information to predict or understand consumer demand. Media Predict *(mediapredict.com)* which relies on UGC to rate manuscripts, television plots, and rock bands, collaborated with Touchstone Books to publish a manuscript (Cohen 2007; Tredinnick 2006). UGC also persuaded Cadbury to reintroduce a discontinued chocolate bar because almost fourteen thousand Facebook members petitioned to bring the bar back (Pfanner 2007).

Second, many social-media websites such as Facebook and TripAdvisor, make money from advertising. These businesses provide services that invite UGC and thrive with increasing participants and interaction. Advertisers spent $2.1 billion in 2010 on these sites, and this is projected to reach $8.3 billion by 2015 (Wasserman 2011). In addition, Facebook and MySpace introduced advertisements tailored to information in user profiles (Stone 2007). For instance, customised advertisements from companies such as Adidas, Kraft, and McDonald's use MySpace's HyperTargeting system that scans and sorts user profiles on interests and demographics (Urstadt 2008). A Malaysian company, Nuffnang, ranked twenty-nine in Malaysia by Alexa, uses a similarly targeted advertising approach to connect brands such as AirAsia, Nokia, and Honda with bloggers within Asia (Alexa 2011; Luk 2011).

Third, users on social media communicate thoughts and experiences through text, photo, and video, transmitting word-of-mouth (WOM) interaction concerning products and services among individuals without any financial incentives (Anderson 1998; Jansen, Zhang, Sobel, and Chowdury 2009; Litvin, Goldsmith, and Pan 2008). Positive WOM can increase visitors, purchases, and customer loyalty (Dey and Sarma 2010; Kim, Lee, and Hiemstra 2004; Ye, Law, and Gu 2009). For example, social media assists potential travellers to plan and anticipate trips, as well as helping experienced travellers recommend and plan return visits (Stevensen 2008). Furthermore, customers gained through WOM give more long-term profit than customers acquired through marketing (Villanueva, Yoo and Hanssens 2008). In a nutshell, social media plays a crucial role in impression management—both directly and indirectly.

An overall observation of the above-mentioned strategies highlights the use of several common impression-management tactics identified by Jones and Pittman (1982) and other unique emerging tactics. For example, communication to create brand awareness and the use of advertisements reflects the use of self-promotion tactics to some extent. The reliance on WOM does reflect a unique tweak to the self-promotion strategy. The change in impression-management strategies via social media remains unclear. There are not many studies that support the transition to different tactics. However, it is undeniable that there is an increasing use in social media to impression-manage by organisations and individuals alike.

Leaders and Social Media: A New Partnership?

Business and political leaders are expected to maintain solid associations with their stakeholders for long-term value. On the other hand, many leaders understand that they need to build close interactions with their followers for highly interdependent goal accomplishment.

Communication on social media via virtual teams synchronises the coordination activities for leaders to disseminate the information to followers in real time.

Social media has transformed leadership style into the next wave of revolution. Leaders today are expected to begin viewing social media as a personal toolbox for improving their practice of leadership (Samuel 2012). According to Brandfog (Ann 2012), social media has become increasingly essential to reinforce the integrity of a leader in managing his or her followers. Hence, it is believed that leaders can refine their practice of leadership by embracing connectivity through social media (Balas, et al. 2011; Samuel 2012).

At present, leaders have begun using social media to manage follower impressions about them. Given that social media allows a social presence that facilitates the forming of impressions of other people about the user (Kaplan and Haenlein 2010), leaders have joined the bandwagon of social media. For example, councillors in the 2010 United Kingdom election engaged social media to enhance their outreach and impression. At the time this was written, the then Gujarat's chief minister, Narendra Modi (now prime minister of India), was approaching 2 million followers on Twitter and was competing head-on for the prime ministerial post against Rahul Gandhi on Facebook (Rai 2013). Politicians such as Barack Obama use social media to reach out to their followers. At the time this was written, Barack Obama had more than 35 million Facebook "likes" for his profile page and about 2 million people talking about his page. Furthermore, the White House has created an official Flickr profile and has nearly five thousand photos on the president (The White House 2012).

We reviewed the social-media sites commonly used by political and business leaders from all over the world. The results of the review are presented in Table 1. As can be seen in Table 1, Facebook, Twitter, Instagram, and blog sites appear to be the preferred venues for personal engagement with stakeholders and followers, by both political and business leaders. In fact, Twitter and Facebook appear to be more commonly used by political leaders than business leaders. One could postulate that business leaders prefer to use specific sites for the company in general, instead of personal sites to share information about the business.

Table 1: Social Media Used by Selected Business and Political Leaders

No.	Name	Position	Social media sites commonly used by leaders							
			Facebook	Twitter	LinkedIn	YouTube	MySpace	Instagram	Blog	Wikipedia
1	Datuk Seri Najib Tun Razak	Prime Minister of Malaysia	√	√	√	√	X	√	√	X
2	Lee Hsien Loong	Prime Minister of Singapore	√	√	√	√	X	√	X	X
3	Datuk Seri Panglima Hishammuddin bin Tun Hussein	Malaysian Minister of Defence	√	√	X	√	X	√	X	X
4	YB Khairy Jamaluddin Abu Bakar	Malaysian Minister of Youth and Sports	√	√	X	√	√	√	√	X
5	Barack Obama	President of the United States	√	√	√	√	√	√	X	X
6	Sheikh Mohammed Bin Rashid Al Maktoum	Prime Minister of the UAE and Ruler of Dubai	√	√	X	√	X	√	X	X
7	Abdullah Guel	President of Turkey	√	√	X	X	√	√	X	X

8	Dato' Seri Abdul Wahid Omar	Minister in the Prime Minister's Department in charge of Financial Affairs	X	X	X	X	X	X	X	X
9	Benigno Aquino III	President of the Philippines	√	√	X	X	X	X	X	X
10	David Cameron	Prime Minister of UK	√	√	√	X	X	X	X	X
11	Bill Gates	Founder, Technology Advisor and Board member of Microsoft Corporation Co-chair, Bill & Melinda Gates Foundation	√	√	√	X	X	X	√	X
12	Jeffrey Cheah Fook Ling	Chairman of the Sunway Group, Malaysia	X	X	X	X	X	X	X	X
13	Tan Sri Anthony Francis "Tony" Fernandes	Group CEO at AirAsia	√	√	√	X	X	X	X	X
14	Satya Nadella	Chief Executive Officer of Microsoft	√	√	√	X	X	X	X	X
15	Anil Ambani	Chairman of Reliance Group, India	X	X	X	X	X	X	X	X
16	Sir Richard Charles Nicholas Branson	Founder of Virgin Group	√	√	√	√	X	√	√	X
17	Dato' Sri Jamaludin Ibrahim	Managing Director/ President & Group Chief Executive Officer of Axiata Group Berhad	X	X	X	X	X	X	X	X

18	Donald John Trump, Sr.	Chairman and President of The Trump Organization	√	√	X	X	X	√	X	X
19	Min-Liang Tan	Co-founder, CEO and Creative Director of Razer USA	√	√	√	√	X	X	X	X
20	Anand Mahindra	Chairman and Managing Director of Mahindra Group	X	√	X	X	X	X	X	X

Note: The information presented in this table was based on a qualitative review of sites used by the leaders until July 2014. Leaders No. 1 to 10 represent political leaders, whereas leaders No.11 to 20 represent business leaders.

With reference to the summary of the types of social media engaged by various leaders, one can conclude that the use of social media by leaders is fairly common. In fact, the adoption of social media appears to be straightforward. However, this new partnership between social media and leadership is not without challenges. Social media has opened a veritable Pandora's box of challenges for leaders, including (but hardly limited to) managing new business models, information overflow (Deiser and Newton 2013), mining for information (Samuel 2012), and so forth. Among these numerous challenges, a leader's impression management through social media deserves to be showered with a great deal of attention.

Fundamentally, leaders should realise that impression management does not work the way it used to. The use of social media such as Facebook or Twitter opens up the path for interaction between leaders and followers. Although leaders may intend to portray a specific image through social media, followers may be able to influence the image, either positively or negatively, through their responses. If there is a flood of negative responses to a post made by the leader, the damage done to the leader's impression-management process can be serious. Therefore, in order to impression-manage effectively, leaders must be aware of the challenges that come with the use of social media.

Social Media: Issues and Challenges for Leaders

"An important element in the co-creation of leadership is through the attributions that followers place upon leaders ... Attributions are created by linking causality to an event" (Nana, Jackson, and Burch 2010, 722). This statement succinctly summarises the essence of the attribution theory. Leaders are public figures. Their behaviours are closely monitored by their followers, peers, competitors, and other stakeholders. Hence, their success is highly dependent on others' perception about their proficiency and support they receive from followers and other important stakeholders.

Whether or not a leader is perceived to be effective depends in part on others' perception about the leader's competency (Yukl 2013). Therefore, leadership and impression management work hand in hand to develop perceptions of leadership effectiveness. However, impression management through social media may be exceptionally challenging because of the "social contagion effect". This effect reflects the act of subconsciously copying the behaviour of others or the "herd mentality" (Vishwanath 2014). For instance, if majority of the followers on a specific social-media site agree or disagree with a posting made on the site, this may influence others to share similar sentiments. With reference to the social contagion effect, it is anticipated that the reaction of followers to a leader's attempt to impression-manage via social media may create an unexpected twist to the perception of leader effectiveness. The following sections discuss some of the pertinent issues that plague leaders attempting to impression-manage through social media.

Unrestricted Freedom

For ages, restriction of freedom was always put in practice to avoid allowing people to say whatever they believed. In the past, people and companies possessed methods of controlling information available about them. Through well-managed public relations, they could control and manage the information that reached others. The present world is a different story altogether with the advent of social media. Social media does not work in a similar manner as press statements or Web pages, in which interaction is limited and leaders are able to control information shared (Deiser and Newton 2013). "Today ... firms have been increasingly relegated to the side lines as mere observers, having neither the knowledge nor the chance or sometimes even the right to alter publically posted comments provided by their customers" (Kaplan and Haenlein 2010, 60).

Many conversations take place over social media without much restrictions. Almost anyone has a podium to express and protest. Everyone has mobile gadgets that allow them to post videos and pictures. Information is shared openly, without fear of repercussion. People share, publicise, and comment on information posted on social media within seconds (Aula 2010; Deiser and Newton 2013). One unforgettable incident involves the revolution that spread throughout the Middle East (Balas et al. 2011). Social media is used to share with the world what is happening. Information spread like wildfire. Unless Internet bans such as the one implemented during Turkey's 2014 elections are imposed (Scott 2014), in many cases leaders have minimal or no control over the speedy dissemination of information.

Social media allows people to gather information about leaders and make subjective interpretations. Their understanding of the subjective truth is then shared with others within their social network, without further verification of whether or not the information is accurate (Aula 2010). The cycle continues with the subjective truth eventually being accepted as collective truth (Aula 2010). This process can be attributed to the false sense of security obtained through the number of members in social-media sites. Members of sites with a large number of followers tend to be much more excited and less fearful than others (Safranek 2012). They are willing to share information without fear of repercussion, because people gain courage through numbers.

Disconnection from Reality

Social media such as Facebook and Twitter seems to project the real world but to what extent it can be assumed as a real time connection remains uncertain. Despite the fact that social media has removed the barriers of time and distance by allowing interaction 24/7 with large pool of people, but then again like any other innovatory transformation, it has bred other threats as well.

Recent studies show that 93 per cent of a leader-member relationship is forged through communication based on text, images, and phrases on social-media sites (Susan 2012). However, this relationship raises several questions: Does such communication represent the actual relationship? Are the leaders and followers focussing on communication quality or quantity? Is the communication legitimate? Are the followers indeed interacting with their leader, or are they being fed with information crafted by a communication agent hired by the leader? In other words, are the relationships forged through social media trustworthy, and can those relationships help create impressions aligned with reality?

Unrestrained optimism can be a reason for disconnection from reality. Users generally create unsubstantiated information irrespective of whether it is true or false (Aula 2010). Such unverified information is later shared by followers who overly trust the leaders and tend to be naïve in taking information found on social-media sites at face value. They do not put in much or even any effort to look for validation, explanation, or proof supporting the messages they have been fed.

With the amount of unverified information circulating via social media, it is challenging to separate the facts from rumours. Leaders' effort to impression-manage may go down a path disconnected from reality. Leaders' postings may be distorted by members who base their comments and opinions on unverified facts. This will then drive other unsuspecting members to trust the majority instead of the leader. At the end of the day, leaders must bear in mind that followers' impressions about the leader may be influenced by unverified information provided by others as well and not merely by the leader's posting on social-media sites.

False Attribution of Leaders' Capabilities

Leaders engage in social media in their quest to create positive impressions about their competence. Some employ tactics such as self-promotion, in which they highlight their contributions to relevant stakeholders. In contrast, there are some deceitful leaders who engage anonymous people or invent customers to craft the desired image for their product (Aula 2010). Regardless of the impression-management techniques employed, most leaders assume they are still able to control people's perception through social media the same way they were able through traditional broadcast media (Deiser and Newton 2012). Sadly, this is not the case.

Online engagement through social media exposes leaders to a range of reputation risks (Aula 2010; Samuel 2012). "On social networks politicians cannot hide from scrutiny and interactivity" (Rai 2013, 13). When employing social media, leaders need to be aware of the risk of false attribution. As mentioned before, social media is a horizontal participatory media that limits the control of a leader (Deiser and Newton 2013). Users will repost messages based on their interpretation of fragments of other users' postings (Aula 2010; Deiser and Newton 2012). Attributions of leaders' capabilities based on social influence may tarnish the reputation of leaders, if those attributions are based on false information. Lack of response by leaders further worsens the scenario (Fallston Group 2012). Some attributions of leaders are exaggerated on social-media sites.

In reality, leaders must realize that attributions formed through social media may not always reflect the actual perception of their followers. It is impossible for leaders to gauge followers' perceptions about their capabilities based on their apparent popularity over social media. For example, during the thirteenth general election in Malaysia, Prime Minister Najib appeared to be very popular on social media, with almost 1.7 million "Likes" on Facebook and Twitter (Bernice 2013). However, these statistics did not translate into a huge landslide win for the ruling coalition, as one would expect based on the huge following through Facebook. Similarly, the opposition coalition political leaders had high ratings for popularity through social media. Despite the impressive popularity, they were unable to wrest the administration of the nation from the ruling coalition.

"Likes" do not reflect the true perception of followers and do not necessarily translate into votes or positive attribution during an election. For example, if a person wants to post on someone's Facebook page, he or she has to "Like" the particular page first. To provide feedback—whether good or bad—about a business service or to engage with a public figure, you have to "Like" them first, irrespective of your actual feelings or intentions. Hence, the number of "Likes" on a page may not truly reveal the number of "Sincere Like". A number of those "Likes" may simply be individuals liking the page just to post unpleasant comments. Many of the accounts on social media have been created by fake users. Malaysia Kini (2013) reveals that 70 per cent of Prime Minister Najib's 1.41 million followers are fake. This means that these followers have few followers or tweets of their own but follow many other Twitter accounts, and the other 15 per cent of Najib's followers were found to be inactive.

Statistics do not always reflect the actual reputation. This does not also mean that if a leader is regularly online, he or she is honestly engaging and sensitive with the followers. The material intention can be that the leaders want to manage the followers' perception rather than really addressing the issues.

Governance of Social Media

Information on social media can be misleading and harmful (The Star Online 2013). In many cases, social media has become a very destructive tool, which scares and damages people unnecessarily. The issue here is: can information posted via social media be governed?

The still-reigning twentieth-century management model that underlines structured processes and control no longer bears any significance in the present era (Deiser and Newton 2012). Leaders and organisations must embrace the fact that they can no longer maintain control over social media, as they were able to do, to some extent, with conventional broadcast media (Deiser and Newton 2012; The Star Online 2013).

Governance of social media should shift towards the active engagement of leaders through social media and the acquisition of a mindset of openness and imperfections. As leaders are no longer able to control or govern responses to a message when it enters a system (Deiser and Newton 2012), they should be prepared to respond in a politically correct manner. This can be seen through the practice of Dell Corporation. With an uncontrollable volume of conversation taking place over the Web about Dell, their management decided that it was impractical to govern social-media communication through a centralized department; instead, employees are trained how to use social media effectively (Fowler 2011).

Similarly, leaders employing social media must be able to transact using the "currencies of social media—co-create and collaborate" (Deiser and Newton 2012). When information gets shared, leaders should carefully consider when to respond and when to let the conversation take its natural course without direct intervention (Deiser and Newton 2012). In some cases, responsible users engage in self-regulation, through which they verify the information before posting it or are vigilant in pointing out inaccurate postings (The Star Online 2013). Hence, governance of social media needs to take on a more indirect approach, instead of relying on rigid rules and regulations that stifle interaction.

Engaging Followers

Leaders who dodge personal interaction for various reasons are likely ineffective leaders, because they will not be able to fulfil the needs of the followers. They must leverage time and resources via delegation to get full physical participation of followers by managing people's perceptions. Followers want the leader to know, care, focus, and cater to possibilities for them to grow. Such engaged leaders secure engaged followers by communicating clear expectations and building collaborative relationships.

There are two schools of thought about the use of social media to engage followers. One emphasises the role of social media in humanising politicians (Maier 2010) and facilitating interaction and relationship-building (Samuel 2012). In contrast, some believe that engagement is not achievable through social media channels, since there is no personal touch with the followers. This school of thought emphasises that social media creates a new challenge altogether—managing the sheer number of followers, while juggling their long list of tasks and responsibilities (Maier 2010, Samuel 2012).

Undeniably, social media breaks the communication barrier and allows leaders to interact closely with their followers. However, the interaction mentioned here does not refer to the mundane one-way information-sharing process (Balas et al. 2011; Samuel 2012). A report from the IBM Institute for Business Value tells that many people do not even consider engaging with leaders via social media (Samuel and Molly 2012). Instead, they believe social media and social networking are about personal connections with friends and family, not for official connection with business and corporate leaders. Therefore, leaders should understand how their presence is perceived in social media. If a leader has an online reputation that does not fit with his or her profile, the leader should acknowledge the situation and make sure he or she has the resources to work with social-media tools to reshape that perception.

Hence, for effective impression management, leaders are expected to "engage" followers through social media. One-way communication is definitely no longer accepted (Balas et al. 2011). Social media has opened up a different network of conversation between followers and leaders (Maier 2010). Hence, leaders should keep their followers in the loop by tweeting relevant links about recent events, getting speeches recorded and posted on YouTube, or having internal blogs through which appreciation for others can be made public (Samuel 2012).

Besides these options to keep followers informed, leaders can raise and debate issues through their social-media sites and provide honest feedback on the points raised by the followers (Maier 2010). In simple words, leaders should be able to harness the power of social media in engaging their followers. Engaged followers will form a positive impression about their leaders.

Conclusion

Many leaders are already leveraging social media as a powerful tool for connecting with followers and building a reputable and trusted relationship. Obviously, there are risks, but avoiding social media is no longer a choice. The century of one-sided communication no longer exists. As a substitute, leaders now have a continuing two-way conversation with the community at large via social media (Santiago and James 2012). Ethics and effective culture take on new standing as followers become de facto examiners and raters of the leader by putting the leader in the public spotlight. Under these circumstances, it is crucial that relevant parties guarantee the necessary resources for leaders to address social-media issues and challenges. Leaders also need to impress and manage followers' perceptions to establish and execute the proper strategy.

References

AirAsia (2011). AirAsia's Social Media Hub. Retrieved 9 September 2011 from *www.airasia.com/my/en/followuson.html*.

Alexa (2011). Top Sites – Malaysia. Retrieved 9 August 2011 from *http://www.alexa.com/topsites/countries/MY*.

Alexa (2013). Global Traffic Rankings. Retrieved 7 April 2013 from *http://www.alexa.com/topsites*.

Alexa (2013). Top Sites – Malaysia. Retrieved 7 April 2013 from *http://www.alexa.com/topsites/countries/MY*.

Anderson, E W (1998). "Customer Satisfaction and Word of Mouth". *Journal of Service Research, 1*(1), 5–17.

Ann, C (2012). *2012 CEO, Social Media and Leadership Survey*. BrandFog.

Aula, P (2010). "Social Media, Reputation Risk, and Ambient Publicity Management". *Strategy and Leadership, 38* (6), 43–49.

Balas, A, et al. (2011). "Social Media and Future of Leadership: Call for Action in the Balkans". *Social Analysis, 1* (2), 154–166.

Bernard, D (2012). *Total Learning*. Retrieved from "What Do Engaged Leaders Excel At?" *http://blogs.terrapinn.com/total-learning/2012/08/13/engaged-leaders-excel/*.

Bernice, L (2013). *Najib and the Social Media Illusion*. Retrieved 8 July 2013 from The Nut Graph: *http://www.thenutgraph.com/najib-and-the-social-media-illusion/*.

Chen, L C P (2009). "Individual Online Impression Management: Self-Presentation on YouTube". *Proceedings of International Conference on Pacific Rim Management*. California.

Cohen, R (2007). "Is There Wisdom in Crowds?" *International Herald Tribune*. Retrieved 14 October 2007 from *http://select.nytimes.com/iht/2007/08/08/opinion/IHT-08edcohen.1.html*.

Constantinides, E, and S J Fountain (2008). "Web 2.0: Conceptual Foundations and Marketing Issues". *Journal of Direct, Data and Digital Marketing Practice, 9*(3), 231–244.

Deiser, R and S Newton (2013). "Six Social Media Skills Every Leader Needs". *McKinsley Quarterly,* available at *http://www.mckinsey.com/insights/ high_tech_telecoms_internet/six_social-media_skills_every_leader_needs.*

Dey, B, and M K Sarma (2010). "Information Source Usage among Motive-Based Segments of Travelers to Newly Emerging Tourist Destinations". *Tourism Management, 31*(3), 341–344.

Emma, M (2010). *Lessons from Election 2010: Local Politics and Social Media.* Local Government Leadership.

Fallston Group (2012). Retrieved 12 April 2012 from Reputation Attack Via Social Media Channel: *http://www.fallstongroup.com/ reputation-attack-via-social-media-channel/.*

Fowler, G A (2011). "Are You Talking to Me? Yes, Thanks to Social Media and the Best Companies Are Listening". *Wall Street Journal, 23,* 25 April 2011.

Hampton, K et al. (2011). "Social Networking Sites and Our Lives". Retrieved 6 July 2011 from *http://pewinternet.org/Reports/2011/ Technology-and-social-networks.aspx.*

Jantos, L, and C Brulhart (2010). "Online Innovations for Swiss Tourism". Lugano, Switzerland: Keynote at Information and Communication Technologies in Tourism 2010 Conference (ENTER).

Johnston, M (2010). "JetBlue Airways: Social Media to the Rescue". Retrieved 16 June 2010 from *http://events.eyefortravel.com/social- media/docs/Case_Study-JetBlue_Airlines.pdf.*

Jones, E E, and T S Pittman (1982). "Toward a General Theory of Strategic Self-Presentation". In J Suls (Ed.), *Psychological Perspective on the Self.* Hillsdale, NJ: Erlbaum, 231–261.

Kaplan, A M, and M Haenlein (2010). "Users of the World, Unite! The Challenges and Opportunities of Social Media". *Business Horizons,* 53(1), 59–68.

Kaplan, A, and M Haenlein, (2012). "Social Media: Back to the Roots and Back to the Future". *Journal of Systems and Information Technology, 14*(2), 101–104.

Leary, M R and R M Kowalski (1990). "Impression Management: A Literature Review and Two-Component Model". *Psychological Bulletin, 107*(1), 34–47.

Maier, E (2010). *Lessons from Election 2010: Local Politics and Social Media.* Local Government Leadership.

Malaysia Kini (2013). "Najib Has Most 'Fake' Twitter Followers, Analysis Finds". Retrieved 15 September 2013 from *http:// my.news.yahoo.com/najib-most-fake-twitter-followers-analysis-finds-075014934.html.*

Malaysian Insider (2013). "Perception Is BN's Biggest Problem, Says Najib". Retrieved 3 June 2013 from *http://www.themalaysianinsider. com/malaysia/article/perception-is-bns-biggest-problem-says-najib.*

McNeill, L (2011). "British Airways Looks for Pilots on YouTube". Retrieved 12 August 2011 from *www.travelmole.com/ stories/1148926.php.*

Mike, M (2012). *N2Growth.* Retrieved 15 September 2013 from The Disconnected Leader: *http://www.n2growth.com/blog/ disconnected-ceo/.*

Nana, E, Jackson, B,, and G S J Burch (2010). "Attributing Leadership Personality and Effectiveness from the Leader's Face: An Exploratory Study". *Leadership and Organisational Development Journal, 31*(8), 720–740.

Pfanner, E (2007). "Consumers Have Voice on Web 2.0". Retrieved 14 October 2007 from *www.iht.com/articles/2007/08/26/business/ brands27.php.*

Rai, S (2013). "Votes and 'Likes': In India's Polarizing Election of 2014 Twitter and Facebook Are Already Winners". *Forbes Asia*, 13.

Safranek, R (2012). "The Emerging Role of Social Media in Political and Regime Change". *Discovery Guides,* available at *http://www.csa. com/discovery guides/discoveryguides_main.php.*

Samuel, A (2012). "Better Leadership through Social Media". *The Wall Street Journal (Asia edition),* available at *http://online.wsj.com/article/ SB10001424052970203753704577255531558650636.html.*

Samuel, G, and W Molly (2012). "The Effects of Leader-Member Exchange on Member Performance in Virtual World Teams". *Journal of the Association for Information Systems, 13,* 861–885.

Santiago, C, and D S James (2012). "Corporate Governance and Social Media; A Brave New World for Board Directors" *The Global Corporate Governance Forum, 27,* 1-16.

Scott, A (2014). "Turkey's YouTube and Twitter Bans Show a Government in Serious Trouble". Retrieved 22 July 2014 from *http://www.theguardian.com/commentisfree /2014/mar/28/ turkey-youtube-twitter-ban-government-trouble*

The Star Online. (2013). *Social Media in Malaysia*. Malaysia: The Star Online.

Stevensen, A (2008). "Managing the Customer Lifecycle". Retrieved 2 March 2009 from *www.tourism2-0.co.uk/profiles/blogs/2021287:BlogPost:1889.*

Stone, B (2007). "MySpace Mines Data to Tailor Advertising". *International Herald Tribune* Retrieved 20 September 2007 from *http://www.nytimes.com/2007/09/18/technology/18iht-social.1.7545453.html.*

Susan, T (2012). "Is Social Media Sabotaging Real Communication?" Retrieved from *http://www.forbes.com/sites/susantardanico/2012/04/30/ is-social-media-sabotaging-real-communication/.*

Urstadt, B (2008). "Social Networking Is Not a Business". *Technology Review, 111*(4), 36–43.

Villanueva, J, Yoo, S, and D M Hanssens (2008). "The Impact of Marketing-Induced versus Word-of-Mouth Customer Acquisition on Customer Equity Growth". *Journal of Marketing Research*, *45*(1), 48–59.

Vishwanath, A (2014). "Diffusion of deception in social media: Social contagion effects and its antecedents". *Information Systems Frontiers*, DOI: *10.1007/s10796-014-9509-2*

Wasserman, T (2011). "Social Media Ad Spending to Hit $8.3B in 2015". Retrieved 12 August 2011 from *http://mashable.com/2011/05/03/social-media-ad-spending-8b/*.

The White House (2012). The White House's Photostream on Flickr. Retrieved 7 April 2013 from *http://www.flickr.com/photos/whitehouse/*.

CHAPTER SEVEN

Media Richness Theory for Social Media Research: Opportunities and Challenges

Noor Akma Mohd Salleh[1] and Sedigheh Moghavvemi[1]

Summary: In this chapter, a meta-review of the media richness theory (MRT), as applied in IS discipline, was conducted using twenty published studies that provided sufficient data to be credible. The results show MRT to be a valid and robust model that has been widely used, one that potentially has wider applicability. The chapter begins by providing the comprehensive explanation of MRT and variables that lead to media choice and media use. The meta-review was conducted based on the following areas: objective, context, and finding. Based on the analysis of the meta-review, several issues were identified that include perception and actual communication performance, the dynamic and evolutionary nature of the media, and media choice and process. These issues have created challenges, which are also described at the end of the chapter.

---

[1] Department of Operation and Management Information System, Faculty of Business and Accountancy, University of Malaya, 50603 Kuala Lumpur, Malaysia.

Introduction

In 1984, Richard L Daft and Robert H Lengel developed media richness theory (MRT) to describe and evaluate communication channels within organisations. MRT originates from contingency theory (Daft and Lengel 1984). The theory was further refined by Daft, Lengel, and Trevino in 1987, by adopting the information-processing theory, together with contingency theory. Since its development, MRT has been used in a great deal of media research, particularly research related to the traditional media, such as newspaper, television, radio, and others. Prior studies in media research use MRT to investigate how organisations cope with communication challenges faced by organisations, particularly challenges related to unclear or confused messages and conflicts in interpretations of messages (Daft and Lengel 1986). More significantly, MRT has been widely used in understanding communication theory. In most communication studies, MRT is used to describe the richness of a communication channel related to media choice, rather than the impact of media use in organisations (Dennis and Kinney 1998). By using MRT, researchers in media and communication studies are able to provide insight and understanding of how individuals select an appropriate channel for communication in their organisations (Lengel and Daft 1989).

With the development of the Internet, new forms of channels have emerged. Facebook, YouTube, Twitter, online videoconferencing, and other social networking sites (SNS) are now becoming the latest channels for organisations and individuals to communicate. For the individuals, these new channels allow them to acquire information, to interact with family and friends, and to provide entertainment and self-satisfaction. Hence, the use of these channels will improve individuals' knowledge, understanding, and interaction skills. Organisations are also taking advantage in using these new communication channels, such as blogs, YouTube, Facebook, and Yelp, to communicate with their business partners, particularly their customers and suppliers. The use of these communication channels provides the means for organisations to achieve their business objectives.

Because of the impact of these new channels both for individuals and organisations, many studies have been conducted to examine the use and impact of these channels, using MRT to provide insight and explanation. For example, MRT is used to address issues related to privacy invasion, communication process, communication performance, and organisational and social impact (He, Zha and Li 2013).

To understand the robustness and significance of MRT, a meta-review on the use of MRT in IS research – particularly the new forms of social-media channels (e.g., Facebook, YouTube, Twitter, online videoconferencing, and other SNS – is discussed. The meta-review is based on selected studies that have been conducted in the last fifteen years. This meta-review focuses on the objectives of the studies, the context, variables, and findings. The analysis of the meta-review will provide insight and understanding about the extent of MRT usage in IS research. From the analysis, issues and challenges are identified which provide a suggestion on how to approach IS research using MRT in the future, particularly in SNS research.

Media Richness Theory

Media richness theory (MRT) postulates that communication channels that are able to convey messages to other in clear and timely manners are considered as having the richness of communication channels. The richness of the communication channels means communications within, and amongst organisations or individuals can overcome different frames of reference and clarify ambiguous issues to promote understanding in a timely manner. MRT also postulates when the communication channels are less rich in the communication within, and amongst organisations and individuals will take a longer time to convey understanding to others. In MRT, the concept of richness in communication channels or media richness is explained as the ability of a communication channel to carry or convey information (Trevino et al. 1987). There are two components of a communication channel's ability to carry information: (1) data-carrying capacity and (2) symbol-carrying capacity (Sitkin, Sutcliffe, and Barrios-Choplin 1992). In MRT, data-carrying capacity refers to the communication channel's ability to transmit information. On the other hand, symbol-carrying capacity refers to the communication channel's ability to transmit not just about the information but also the information about the individuals who are communicating amongst themselves. MRT implies that a sender should select a communication channel that contains appropriate richness to communicate the desired message (Lengel and Daft 1989). Hence, the most immediate and profound application of MRT provides insight and understanding of how senders of messages decide in choosing the appropriate communication channels.

According to media richness theory (MRT), all communication channels possess certain characteristics or capabilities that trigger the richness of these communication channels (Daft et al. 1987). As such, MRT places communication media on a continuous scale that represents the richness of a medium. In other words, MRT focuses on the ability of a channel to adequately communicate a complex message (Carlson and Robert 1999). In MRT, assumption is made that a simple message such as arrangement of meeting time and venue within an organisation can be communicated using a short e-mail. However, for a more detailed message, such as a message about an employee's work performance and expectations, then the message would be better communicated through face-to-face interaction. Hence, MRT postulates that the more ambiguous and uncertain a task is, the richer format of communication channels is needed to suit the message or task.

In MRT, the main characteristics or capabilities that make communication channels more or less rich include the following:

- the capability of organisations providing immediate feedback
- the capability of organisations to transmit multiple cues within organisations
- the capability of organisations in using variety of language
- the capability of organisations of having personal focus related to the messages.

For example, when organisations use a telephone as their communication channel to convey the message, it will be conveyed without the reproduction of visual social cues such as gestures. As such, a telephone message is less rich compared to videoconferencing as a communication channel, because unlike a telephone message, conveying the message through videoconferencing, to some extent, the senders can also communicate gestures. With the development of the Internet, the use of only e-mails to convey the message can create the problem of equivocality in organisations, as it will be less rich.

By understanding the characteristics or capabilities that trigger the richness of communication channels, the theory is used to guide organisations to choose a communication channel that reduces equivocality in a message. The more equivocal a message, the more unclear the message will be, thus creating a difficulty for the message to be decoded by its receivers. In the case of greater equivocal message, organisations need more cues and data to decode and understand that message. Daft and Lengel (1986) argue that with richness elements in any communication channel, ambiguous or equivocal messages can be communicated and understood quickly by individuals. MRT argues that performance improves when team members use "richer" media for equivocal tasks.

Findings from prior studies using MRT provide understanding of the effect of media richness in the decision made by individuals in choosing the appropriate communication channels amongst team members, specifically, the use of computer-mediated and video communication. The MRT explains that media richness is usually dependent on a multiplicity of cues and immediacy of feedback; individuals perceive differences in richness due to both multiple cues and immediate feedback. However, MRT indicates that matching richness to task equivocality did not improve decision quality, decision time, consensus change, or communication satisfaction. As such, prior studies have adopted and adapted MRT for more complex tasks (Leonard, Brands, Edmondson, and Fenwick 1998).

As shown in Figure 1, the MRT conceptual framework consists of axes representing equivocality from low to high and uncertainty from low to high. In the model, both low equivocality and low uncertainty represent levels of clear and well-defined situations. On the contrary, the high equivocality and high uncertainty represent ambiguous events that need clarification. Furthermore, the framework describes communication channels together with the characteristics and abilities of the communication channels, in order to reproduce information sent by organisations and/or individuals over these communication channels without losing or distorting a message.

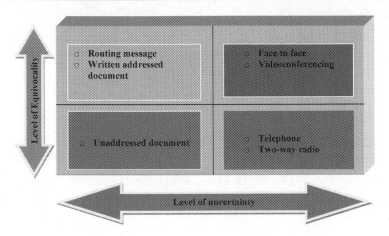

Figure 1: The Framework of Media Richness Theory

The conceptual framework of MRT indicates that richer media is better suited for equivocal, non-routine messages, while leaner media are better suited for unequivocal, routine messages (Daft and Lengel 1989). Although less-rich media may not solve equivocal situations, they do reduce uncertainty. This postulation is based on the argument that less-rich media could help prevent individuals from providing too much information and superfluous messages that contribute to uncertainty. Hence, MRT recognises the contribution of the less-rich communication channels' senders of messages are often forced to use less-rich methods of communication. MRT highlights that any senders of messages using less-rich communication channels should understand the limitations of that medium, particularly on the issues of immediate feedback, multiple cues, message tailoring, and emotions (Newberry 2001).

Meta-Review of Media Richness Theory

Methodology

Twenty papers (see Table 1) related to media richness theory were selected from different top journals from various disciplines for the last fifteen years. The meta-review covers the following topics.

- Objective of the study
- Context and setting
- Variables
- Findings

Table 1: Meta-Review of the Selected Papers

Authors (Year)	Objective	Context	Communication channel	Variables	Findings
El-Shinnawy and Markus (1997)	Investigate reason for choosing electronic mail versus voice mail and test them amongst users of both media in the corporate headquarters of a large company.	employees	electronic mail, voice mail	Level of media richness: richness, richer, and less richness	The low and high level of richness predicts employees choice of channel behaviour.
Dennis and Kinney (1998)	Examine the effect of "richer" media for equivocal tasks on performance.	Team member	Various communication channels	Multiple cues, immediate feedback, Equivocal task	Multiplicity of cues and immediate feedback increases performance for more equivocal tasks
Sheer and Chen (2004)	Investigate the role of relational and self-presentational goals on the interaction between manager-subordinate when messages differ in valence.	Manager	Various communication channels	Relational, self-presentational, equivocality, richer media,	Self-presentational goals predict media choice when messages are negative, relational goals and complexity predicts media choice.
Cable, Yang, and Yu (2006)	Identify perceptions of media richness and credibility.	Manager; MBA job seeker		Media richness, media credibility; job seekers' image beliefs; companies' projected images	Richness and credibility perceptions enhance job seekers' initial beliefs about firms' images.

Shepherd and Marrz Jr. (2006)	Examine the effect of the low and high level of richness of communication amongst students.	Student	Online communication (distance learning), technology	Satisfaction, richness of media Communication, interaction	Satisfaction, richness of media and Communication and interaction plays significant role in online communicaion
Chen, Chen, and Kazman (2007)	Understand the impact of e-CRM "touch" design perceived by e-customers on their intention to return after the initial visit.	e-consumer	e-CRM	Media richness, perceived interactivity, attitudes towards the system, intention to return, perceived ease of use and perceived usefulness	Perceived ease of use has significant impact on the intention to return. Perceived usefulness directly impacts both decision satisfaction and attitude toward the system.
Yih Chao and Chen (2010)	Examine the impact of social loafing perceived risk in group cohesion, effect.	Consumer	Online community sites	Offline activities, anonymity, social ties, social loafing, group cohesion, media richness, perceived knowledge, quality risk	Social ties a ad perceived risk are importa nt components of social loafing. Social loafing has a negative effect on users' group cohesion. Anonymity, offline activities, knowledge quality, and media richness affect social ties and perceived risk.
Aljukhadar, Senecal, and Ouellettre (2010)	Investigate the effect of media richness on retailer trust and behavioural intentions.	Retailers	e-store social presence,	Media richness, social presence, retailer trust, agent trust, behavioural intentions, retailer trust, purchase intentions	Social media richness, trust and perceived risk as important variables that affect intentions,.

Yu and Yang (2010)	Evaluate the various media richness of message delivery methods in m-learning environment.	Students	SMS, e-mail, and RSS in m-learning environment	Content richness, content accuracy, content adaptability, content timeliness	Content richness, accuracy, adaptability, timeliness affect the effectiveness of message delivery using e-mail, RS, SMS.
Sukoco and Wann (2011)	Identify and test consumer cognitive and affective responses in advertisement context.	Consumer	Advertisement sites	Tele-presence, Interactivity, Media Richness, Search Attributes, Experience Attributes,	Tele-presence, Interactivity, Media Richness, are significant when the product is dominated by search attributes rather than experience attributes.
Yates and Paquette (2011)	Investigate determinants that influence knowledge sharing, reuse, and decision-making.	Consumer	Social media technologies	Social media, knowledge sharing, decision-making	Social media had an impact on individuals within an emergency response organisation.
Dewan and Ramaprasad (2011)	Examine the relationship between new media, old media, and sales, in the context of the music industry.	Consumer	Blog	Buzz, music sales, audio play	Audio play has a positive effect future sales of songs and albums. Blog buzz has negative effect on future song sales.
Oestreicher-Singer, Zalmanson (2013)	Examine the relations between social content consumption, users' participation patterns, and their willingness to pay, using data from last.fm.	Radio listener	Radio	Premium services; online communities; propensity,	Strategic view rather than technocentric view of social media for digital firms that remain viable in a world of "fermium".

Oh, Agrawal, and Rao (2013)	Investigate t conditions for collective social reporting function as a community intelligence mechanism.	Individuals	Twitter, rumour mill	Social reporting, social information processing, social crisis, extreme community intelligence	Anxious Twitter message which is more likely to be a rumour than an anxiety-free message. Ambiguous Twitter message is more likely to be a rumour than real-situation Twitter message.
Jiang, Cheng, and Choi (2013)	Examine the antecedents of privacy concerns and social rewards.	Student	Synchronous online	Social interactions privacy concerns, privacy-protective behaviour, social rewards, self-disclosure, misrepresentation	Perceived anonymity and perceived intrusiveness affect both privacy concerns and social rewards. The higher the perceived anonymity of self, the lower individuals' privacy concerns. The higher the level of perceived media richness, the higher the increases social rewards.
Huang, Baptista, and Galliers (2013)	Examine the effect of social-media inquiry on organisational rhetorical practices.	Consumer	Social-networking sites	Rhetorical practices, intra-organisational communication, social media, interpretive	Multivocality, increasing reach and richness in communication facilitate the shaping of organisational rhetorical practices via social media enablement.

Laroche, Habibi, and Richard (2013)	Understand how social media elements in the context of customer-centric model and brand loyalty.	Consumer	Social-networking sites	Brand communities, focal customer, brand trust, brand loyalty	Brand trust mediates the effect between brand community and brand loyalty.
Wu and Li (2013)	Analyse unstructured text content on Facebook and Twitter.	Consumer	Facebook and Twitter	Competitive intelligence, actionable intelligence, text mining	Competitive intelligence, actionable intelligence, text mining have greater impact in Facebook than in Twitter.
Shen, Cheung and Lee(2013)	Examine social group category on a target collective behaviour.	Consumer	Short instant messaging (SMS).	We-intention, subjective norm, group norm, social identity, perceived critical mass	Subjective norm, group norm, social identity, perceived critical mass affect the We-intention. Thus, individuals with similar values or goals tend to develop we-intentions to use instant messaging (SMS).
Phang and Zhang (2013)	Examine the level of participation attained in a social media platform.	Consumer	Social networking sites	Social media participation, user interaction, network structural properties, consumption intention, participation attained, reciprocity, in- degree centralization, out- degree centralization, betweenness centralization, centralization.	Participation level is influence by interaction patterns high inclusiveness and betweenness centralisation. Meanwhile the participation level affect consumption intention

Meta-Review Analysis

Objectives Using Media Richness Theory

From the meta-review, researchers use media richness theory (MRT) to achieve the following objectives.

Privacy Invasion

Prior studies have used MRT to examine the key determinants that influence perceived privacy (e.g., Jiang, Cheng, and Choi 2013). In addition, the influence of interactivity and the effect of positive and negative information on privacy are also examined by uses of social networking (e.g., Aljukhadar, Senecal, and Ouellette 2010).

Communication Process

Analysis of the meta-review also indicated that MRT is used to investigate the communication processes of social media in the media capability to form communication groups. The theory was also used to investigate the dominant role of social media in terms of the proximity of communication partners or groups, related to the urgency of the situation and time constraints (Chen, Chen, and Kazman 2007; Yu and Yang 2010). MRT was also used in prior research to test the relationship between the communications (such as e-mail) on social communication (e.g., Yu and Yang 2010; Sukoco and Wann 2011).

Communication Performance

Prior studies investigated in this meta-review also indicated the use of MRT in examining firm performance. The meta-review reveals that MRT has been used to explore the relationship between high-content richness such as accuracy timeliness, adaptability, and communication performance. For example, MRT has been used to examine the organisational impact of the fashion phenomenon in information technology (e.g., Huang, Baptista, and Galliers 2013). Some researchers use MRT to argue how the richness and immediacy of feedback increases team communication performance (e.g., Dennis and Kinney 1998). By using MRT, researchers are able to identify how communication performance improves via the greater extent of equivocal tasks than less-equivocal tasks (e.g., El-Shinnawy and Markus, (1997; Dennis and Kinney 1998; Sheer and Chen 2004).

Organisational and Social Impact

MRT is also used to investigate the impact of social media on organisation and society. From the meta-review, a majority of studies used MRT to examine the usage of Facebook and its impact on climate change amongst employees. The aims of these studies are to demonstrate that a lean medium such as Facebook can be effectively used for an equivocal task, such as raising environmental awareness (Oestreicher-Singer and Zalmanson 2013). Some researchers used MRT to explore the state of current knowledge about online social networks (OSNs) and their role in precipitating changes in existing market structures (e.g., Dave, Yates, and Paquette 2011).

Context of the Study

The meta-review reveals how MRT has been used in different contexts. For the purpose of this meta-review, this paper analyses the literature in two main timeframes: prior to 2000 and after 2000. Most studies prior to 2000 focus on managers and executives in organisations using communications media to communicate with their subordinates. In contrast, most studies conducted after 2000 focus on online individuals, online users and employees of the organisation. The focus on different contexts between these two timeframes is related to the advances in Internet technologies. Most literature on communications media using MRT are about e-mail, face-to-face, videoconference, telephone, voicemail, electronic phone (chat), asynchronous groupware, synchronous groupware, letters, and memos (Sukoco and Wann 2011;Yates and Paquette 2011; Oestreicher-Singer and Zalmanson 2013; Agrawal and Rao 2013; Huang, Baptista, and Galliers 2013). Most prior research is focused on these forms of communication channels because after 2000, these forms of communication media have been made available for all individuals and employees, not just managers and top executives.

Constructs/Variables

The meta-review indicates that most of the constructs from MRT are adapted to the context of studies. The main constructs of MRT, such as content, interaction, and maintenance, are the prominent constructs being used to investigate issues on privacy, communication process, communication performance, and organisational and social impact. The meta-review shows that content richness and interaction richness are most significant in identifying and answering all the issues. Apart from the main constructs in MRT, some studies have used other constructs of MRT. Examples of constructs include technology collaboration, media capabilities, communication designers, and corporate reputation. On that note, Valacich et al. (1994) extended the MRT by proposing the theory of media synchronicity, which postulates there are two primary processes in the group-communication process: conveyance and convergence. According to this theory, apart from the elements of media-richness constructs, the conveyance and convergence process are relatively important, regardless of task-outcome communication processes and task-outcome objectives. The theory also posits that media have a set of capabilities, which are dominant, particularly in addressing each type of communication process. As such, in the theory of media synchronicity, Valancich et al. introduce constructs such as parallelism, symbol variety, and rehearsability. This theory also proposes that apart from the main construct of MRT.

Findings from the Use of Media Richness Theory

The meta-review indicates the use of MRT in selected literature that addresses issues related to privacy invasion, communication process, communication performance, and organisational and social impact.

Lan and Sie (2010) use MRT to examine Facebook users in Taiwan. By using MRT, they were able to identify and examine the antecedent of machine interaction and interpersonal interaction. Their study indicates the importance of content richness and content accuracy in the Facebook among Facebook users when these users interact with the machine, in this case the information technology. However, in relation to interpersonal interaction, Facebook users did usually focus on the media richness. MRT was also used by Bulsiewicz (2003) to explore how environmental brand experience can be used to promote digital publishing content. By using MRT, Bulsiewicz was able to demonstrate how environmental brand experience can influence the adoption and use of the hybrid design development method. His study was able to provide insight into how, by media, richness would improve the design process of products or services.

Meanwhile, Sheer and Chen (2004) use MRT by proposing a manager-subordinate interaction in the communication process between manager and their subordinate. This manager-subordinate interaction is important in the communication processparticularly when messages differ in valence relational and also when self-presentational goals are very relevant. By using MRT, Sheer and Chen provide insight into how managers in ambiguous and superfluous conditions (i.e., under deceptive conditions) perceive a negative message as more complex than a positive message, particularly when equivocality is constant. It seems that in a state of constant equivocation, managers are more likely to choose richer media to convey a positive message than a negative message. MRT demonstrates that when a negative message is being conveyed in the state of equivocation, managers will perceive less anticipated communication effectiveness.

Managers will also have less ability to maintain a good relationship with subordinates and have less ability to project a good image. Using MRT, Sheer and Chen also demonstrated that managers experience a high degree of anxiety when communicating a negative message, thus impacting the manager-subordinate relationship. On the other hand, MRT shows that if there is no difference in message valence, then the complexity of the message would be a better predictor of the manager's choice of media. Thus, MRT holds relevant when messages are positive, particularly in relational goals, which have some impact on managers' media choice.

On that note, Dennis, Kinney, and Hung (1999) argue that MRT can be used to examine communication performance. They postulate that communication performance amongst team members can be improved when team members use "richer" media for equivocal tasks. In this scenario, communication performance of team members is improved by multiple increases in cues. They also argue that if multiplicity of cues increases to a greater extent, it will improve communication performance for equivocal tasks, rather than fewer equivocal tasks. At the same time, as immediacy of feedback increases, the communication will also improve, particularly for more equivocal tasks.

Dennis, Kinney, and Hung (1999) highlighted that MRT has some limitations, particularly when testing "new media" such as computer-mediated communication. Using MRT as the basis, Dennis (1999) extends the theory by proposing the theory of media synchronicity, which postulates that regardless of whether the task is an outcome communication process and outcome objectives. group communication processes are composed of conveyance and convergent processes, Using this extended theory, Dennis, Kinney, and Hung provide insight that media usually has a set of capabilities that play a dominant role when addressing each type of communication channel. Using the theory of media synchronicity, they demonstrate how communication performance can be enhanced, particularly when media capabilities are aligned with these processes (i.e., conveyance and convergence).

Due to the current debate about the antecedents of media choice on the concerns of the explanatory power of various theories, particularly the MRT and social influence approaches. Subsequently, Webster and Trevino (1995) use MRT together with social influence theory (SIT) in an attempt to determine which of these two theories best explains people's choices of communication media. They found that MRT and SIT are complementary rather than competing.

Lan and Sie (2010) use MRT to examine the key determinants that influence perceived interactivity and perceived privacy in the environment social-network site (Facebook) in Taiwan. They identify four constructs that include content timeliness, content richness, content accuracy, and content adaptability in MRT, to explore the relationship amongst perceived interactivity, perceived privacy, and user behaviour. They find that all constructs play important roles as antecedents of machine interaction and interpersonal interaction, especially content richness and content accuracy. However, these constructs only act as partial antecedents of online privacy invasion and perceived privacy risk beliefs. The research also reveals that users are still inclined to use SNSs with positive attitudes. However, they may choose other social media that have more attractive features or better privacy settings because of online privacy invasion and privacy risk beliefs.

Dennis, Fuller, and Valacich (2008) employed the theory of synchronicity proposed by Valacich et al. (1994) to examine communication performance. They found that media supporting lower synchronicity should result in better communication performance. Their study also revealed that for convergence processes, use of media supporting higher synchronicity should result in better communication performance. On the other hand, for conveyance processes, use of media supporting lower synchronicity should result in better communication performance. Wang (2010) examined some of the important organisational impacts of the fashion phenomenon in IT, using MRT. In his study, he demonstrates how MRT explains the diffusion of IT innovation in fashion phenomena at the middle phase of diffusion. The results explain that the diffusion of IT innovation in fashion can be a legitimate organisation and as a leader, regardless of communication performance improvement. The findings also extend the use of institutional theory from its usual focus that is on take-for-granted practices to fashion to be one of the sources of social approval.

Considering the findings of the meta-review, it is clear that MRT is used in various contexts and settings. To a certain extent, the findings of prior studies on MRT provide insights and understanding related to communication media. From the findings, it seems that content richness, accuracy, adaptability, and timeliness will improve communication amongst groups and team members. In addition, by using MRT, researchers are able to examine how the extent of media-content richness such as accuracy, adaptability, and timeliness influence privacy. It seems that the lack of media richness and interactivity creates privacy invasion. In other words, when content is lacking in accuracy and timeliness, the users of communication media will perceive that their privacy is being compromised. Media richness theory also assists in explaining how the extent of content richness affects social interaction between groups and teams.

MRT is also employed to demonstrate the influence on political opinion and voter participation (MI 1999). Through a longitudinal study, two forms of media (newspaper and television) were examined in their coverage of war news. Drawing from MRT, the study reveals that certain forms of media, particularly television, have a greater informational impact on viewers. Subsequently, the choice of television as communication channels is to increase viewer cognitive information and action. In contrast, MRT also demonstrates that too much attention to television campaigns creates a media saturation level. This result suggests that quality, not quantity, is an important factor for political reasoning and action.

MRT was also used to study the usage of Facebook that may increase climate-change awareness amongst employees (Ali 2011). Results indicate that reading the newspaper or paying attention to campaign material in newspapers has no effect on subsequent political opinion, ideology, or turnout. Prior studies using MRT also demonstrate how Facebook as a lean medium can be effectively used for an equivocal task, such as raising environmental awareness. MRT is also able to demonstrate that Facebook is one example of a lean medium that creates effective communication, particularly in engaging employees once messages are distributed to them.

From the meta-review, prior researchers have identified limitations to MRT and propose a theory of media synchronicity to address the limitations of MRT. With the theory of media synchronicity, apart from content-richness construct, other constructs such as parallelism, rehearsability, complexity, and conflict explain the group/team communication performance. The meta-review also indicates several issues that need to be addressed if one is to use MRT and/or media synchronicity theory in the area of social-networking sites, such as Facebook and YouTube.

Issues and Challenges

Actual versus Perceived Communication Performance

A majority of prior studies examine the *perception* of communication performance, rather than the actual performance. Communication performance related to performing a task, as such, is more a task nature rather than a perception nature. Therefore, the direction future research should go is in examining the nature of communication tasks used. In other words, more research needs to be conducted on comparing different types of tasks, such as communications tasks and decision-making tasks, to determine whether media richness theory only applies to communications tasks. However, for IS researchers, particularly in social-networking sites, more studies of media richness theory (MRT) should be explored to examine actual performance, rather than just perceptions.

Therefore, the challenges for future research would be to:

- find valid and reliable measurements for actual communication performance constructs
- identify actual related tasks that directly impact the actual performance
- identify effective points of time to measure actual performance related to the task

- identify sources of the data (primary or secondary data – the most appropriate way of data collection

Nature of Media

Issues and Challenges

The nature of the media is very dynamic and evolutionary. Attention needs to be placed on creating interactivity functionality in the media communication website. The issues would involve investigating the pressures induced by online social networks (OSNs). Another issue would be how to empirically address incumbents' responses over time, due to the dynamic and evolutionary movements that entail such interactions.

Therefore, the challenges for future research would identify pressures induced by

- competitors (in term of products, barriers, new entrances)
- changes in environment (precipitating events, policy)
- changes in technology (IS innovation, technological change)
- organisation (implementation of new policy, technology, process, business activity).

Context and Setting

Issues and Challenges

Choosing one single medium for any task may prove less effective than choosing a medium or set of media the group uses at different times in performing the task, depending on the current communication process (convey or converge). Media switching may be most appropriate. The successful completion of most tasks involving more than one individual requires both conveyance and convergence processes; thus, communication performance will be improved when individuals use a variety of media to perform a task, rather than just one medium. Therefore, if the successful completing of the tasks involved more than one individual, apart from choosing the set of medium for communication performance, one need to pay attention on privacy setting of the communication medium for the individual.

Therefore the challenges for future research would be to

- choose two or more media (Facebook and Twitter)
- identify a specific task to a specific medium (operational task and managerial task)
- identify criteria for privacy settings (security features).

Discussion and Conclusion of Meta-Review

The meta-review shows that media richness theory (MRT) makes distinctions between media high in richness and media low in richness. The extent of richness is defined based on the number of the cues a medium passes on and how easy it is to give feedback. The more cues can be passed on and the easier it is to give feedback, the higher the information richness (Daft and Lengel 1984). From the meta-review, it seems that MRT is used by IS researchers to examine how communication process and performance are achieved. IS researchers have used the theory in different settings and contexts. It seems that managers prefer information-rich media to information-poor media for complex messages and that they prefer information-poor media to information-rich media for simple messages. Other factors that play important roles are the distance between sender and receiver, the number of receivers, social influences, and symbolic cues of media.

MRT provides a framework for describing a communication medium's ability to reproduce the information sent over it without loss or distortion. For example, a phone call will not be able to reproduce visual social cues such as gestures. This form of a medium makes it less rich (as a communication medium) than videoconferencing, which is able to communicate gestures, to some extent, but richer than e-mail. Specifically, MRT states that the more ambiguous and uncertain a task is, the richer format of media suits it.

In conclusion, there are issues and challenges to MRT. Future research should concentrate on these issues and tackle the challenges of using MRT, specifically in the social-networking sites (SNS) if the researcher wants to have conclusive results and insights.

References

Ali, M S S (2011). "The Use of Facebook to Increase Climate Change Awareness among Employees". International Conference on Social Science and Humanity (IPEDR), v. 5.

Carlson, John R and Robert W Zmud (1999). "Channel Expansion Theory and the Experiential Nature of Media Richness Perceptions". *The Academy of Management Journal* 42 (2): 153–170.

Chen, Q, Chen, H M, and R Kazman (2007). "Investigating Antecedents of Technology Acceptance of Initial eCRM Users beyond Generation X and the Role of Self-Construal". *Electronic Commerce Research,* 7(3–4), 315–339.

Daft, R L and R H Lengel (1984). "Information Richness: A New Approach to Managerial Behavior and Organizational Design". *Research in Organizational Behavior* (Homewood, IL: JAI Press) 6:191–233.

_____ (1986). "Organizational Information Requirements, Media Richness, and Structural Design". *Management Science* 32(5), 554–571.

Daft, R L, Lengel, R H, and L K Trevino (1987). "Message Equivocality, Media Selection, and Manager Performance: Implications for Information Systems". *MIS Quarterly,* 355–366.

Dennis, A R, Fuller, R M, and Joseph S. Valacich (2008). "Media, Tasks, and Communication Processes: A Theory of Media Synchronicity". *MIS Quarterly,* v. 32 (3), 575–600.

Dennis, A R and S T Kinney (1998). "Testing Media Richness Theory in New Media: The Effects of Cues, Feedback, and Task Equivocality". *Information Systems Research* 9 (3): 256–274.

Dennis, A R, Kinney, S T, and Yu-Ting Caisy Hung (1999). "Gender Differences in the Effects of Media Richness". *Small Group Research,* v. 30 (4), 405–437.

Dennis, A R, and J S Valacich (1999). "Rethinking Media Richness: Towards a Theory of Media Synchronicity". In *Proceedings of the 32nd Hawaii International Conference on System Sciences*, Los Alamitos, CA: IEEE Computer Society Press, Volume 1.

He, W, Zha, S, and L Li (2013). "Social Media Competitive Analysis and Text Mining: A Case Study in the Pizza Industry". *International Journal of Information Management* 33 (2013) 464– 472.

Inter-University Consortium for Political and Social Research [distributor], Ann Arbor, MI (1999). doi:10.3886/ICPSR06067.v2

Lan, Y F and Y S Sie (2010). "Using RSS to Support Mobile Learning Based on Media Richness Theory". *Computers & Education,* 55(2), 723–732.

Lengel, R H and R L Daft (1989). "The Selection of Communication Media as an Executive Skill". *The Academy of Management Executives:* Vol. 2, No. 3, 225–232.

Leonard, D A, et al. (1998). "Virtual Teams: Using Communications Technology to Manage Geographically Dispersed Development Groups". In Bradley, S P and R L Nolan (Eds.), *Sense and Respond— Capturing Value in the Network Era, Client Distribution Services.* Boston, MA, 285–298.

Newberry, Brian (2001). "Media Richness, Social Presence and Technology Supported Communication Activities in Education". http://learngen. org/resources/module/lgend101_norm1/200/210/211_3.html. Retrieved 2007-09-04.Sheer, V C and L Chen (2004). "Improving Media Richness Theory: A Study of Interaction Goals, Message Valence, and Task Complexity in Manager-Subordinate Communication". *Management Communication Quarterly,* v. 18(1), 76–93.

Shiue, Y C, Chiu, C M, and C C Chang (2010). "Exploring and Mitigating Social Loafing in Online Communities". *Computers in Human Behavior,* 26(4), 768–777.

Simon, S J and S C Peppas (2004). "An Examination of Media Richness Theory in Product Web Site Design: An Empirical Study". *Info: The Journal of Policy, Regulation and Strategy for Telecommunications, Information and Media,* 6(4), 270–281.

Sitkin, S, Sutcliffe, K, and J Barrios-Choplin (1992). "A Dual-Capacity Model of Communication Media Choice in Organizations." *Human Communication Research,* 18(4), 563–598.

Trevino, L, Lengel, R, and R Daft (1987). "Media Symbolism, Media Richness, and Media Choice in Organizations". *Communications Research,* 14(5), 553–574.

Valacich, J S, Dennis, R A, and T Connolly (1994). "Idea Generation in Computer-Based Groups; A New Ending to an Old Story". *Organizational Behavior and Human Decision Process,* 57, 448–467.

Wang, P (2010). "Chasing the Hottest IT: Effects of Information Technology Fashions on Organizations". *MIS Quarterly,* 34 (1), 63–85.

Webster, J and K L Trevino (1995). "Rational and Social Theories as Complementary Explanations of Communication Media Choices: Two Policy-Capturing Studies". *The Academy of Management Journal,* v. 38 (6), 1544–1572.

CHAPTER EIGHT

Social Innovation through Social Media

Shamshul Bahri[1] and Ali Fauzi Ahmad Khan[2]

Summary: Social innovation is an activity taken by society to enhance the well-being of its members. Some of the activities include shaping political views, assisting minorities, and reducing poverty. However, social innovation through social media is an area that has remained largely unexplored, although many groups of people have undertaken initiatives that fall under the concept. In this chapter, two Malaysian examples are presented to demonstrate relatively successful social innovations. For these initiatives to be successful, certain challenges need to be overcome.

[1]   Shamshul Bahri, PhD, Department of Operations and MIS, Faculty of Business and Accountancy, University of Malaya, 50603 Kuala Lumpur, Malaysia.
[2]   Department of Information Systems, Faculty of Computer Sciences and Information Technology, University of Malaya, 50603 Kuala Lumpur, Malaysia.

Social Innovation

There are many activities that fall under "social innovation". Those activities include shaping political views, tackling the negative effect of greater urbanization, assisting minorities, reducing poverty, and providing healthcare facilities to the most deprived people in society. Unfortunately, the term "social innovation" is difficult to define. Loosely, it can be defined as activities initiated by those in a society to enhance the well-being of its members.

In other words, social innovation is an initiative from the people, by the people, and for the people. This kind of innovation is different from business organisation. The ability of Apple Corporation to come up with useful and distinct information technologies is an example of business innovation. The differences between social and business innovation are highlighted in Table 1.

Table 1: Comparison between Social and Business Innovation

The Differences	Social Innovation	Business Innovation
Source of the innovation	The innovation is initiated by society, which includes local community and non-profit groups.	The innovation is initiated by business organisations.
Aim of the innovation	The aim is to increase the well-being of the society.	The aim is to increase the revenue and eventually the profits of the organisations.
Promotion of innovation	The initiatives are not promoted through mainstream media, thus largely unknown, except to those who are involved.	The initiatives are often promoted through mainstream media, therefore are often known by a large number of people.

The similarity between the two types of innovation lies in the main stakeholder: the people. The aim of social innovation is to increase the well-being of the people targeted for the initiative. For example, the aim of a crime-prevention initiative is to raise awareness amongst the people about how crime could occur, in order for them to be more vigilant when they are in public spaces. On the other hand, the aim of business innovation is to attract people to purchase products and services offered by business organisations. For example, Apple designed its latest iPhone 5s to be able to read and recognise thumbprints, in order to attract more people to purchase the smartphone.

Studies on Social Innovation and Social Media

Many studies have been conducted on social innovation. Most of these studies were aimed at enhancing society's well-being. For example, Alzugaray (2012) conducted a study on how to increase social inclusion; Edwards (2012) conducted a study on how to empower citizens; while Jensen (2013) conducted a study on how to enhance life opportunities.

These studies differed in terms of context and method employed to enhance society's well-being. For example, Jensen's 2013 study was conducted in a residential home, while Oliveira's 2012 study was conducted in a deprived urban subgroup of society. In terms of method, Alzugaray (2012) proposed some innovative projects, while Edwards (2012) proposed a living lab methodology as socially innovative methods to enhance society's well-being.

Whilst many studies have been conducted on social innovation, studies on the use of social media for social innovation have been scarce. The implications of these studies have also been limited. For example, Choi et al. (2012) introduced new methods to analyse social-media data of online innovation communities in South Korea. On the other hand, Gladwell (2011) studied the impact of protests through social media. He argued that there is no evidence that protesters can challenge governments directly through social media.

The limited number of studies on the use of social media for social innovation is both unfortunate and surprising. It is unfortunate because social media presents so many possibilities for enhancing social well-being. It is surprising because there are many instances where social media has been used to enhance a society's quality of life. In Malaysia alone, a number of social-innovation activities have taken place to achieve the noble aim of improving society's well-being. Two of those initiatives will be described in the next section.

The Use of Social Media for Social Innovation

The Use of Social Media to Enhance Political Awareness

The "Pakatan Rakyat" (the People's Coalition or PR) is a coalition of three different parties: Parti Keadilan Rakyat (the People's Justice Party or PKR), the Democratic Action Party (DAP), and Parti Islam SeMalaysia (the Malaysian Islamic Party or PAS). The three parties used to contest the general election individually. Then, in 2008, the three parties decided to cooperate, to ensure there would be a one-to-one fight with the ruling party, Barisan Nasional (the National Coalition). The coalition proved successful in 2008 when it managed to deny the ruling party the two-thirds majority it had enjoyed since the country received independence from the British in 1957.

One of the biggest difficulties faced by PR is in disseminating its arguments to the people. The coalition did not enjoy the large coverage received by the ruling party in the mainstream print and electronic media. The Watching the Watchdog media-monitoring project for the

13ᵗʰ Malaysia's General Election (GE13) GE13 found that citizens of the country were deprived of receiving fair and objective information about the political parties in the lead-up to the elections. PR received the highest negative mentions of 68 per cent in mainstream media and faced obstructions to convey their political message and arguments on this platform. As a consequence, PR found it hard to convey its political awareness message to the people. The message urges the Malaysian citizen to take an active role in the democratic process by voicing out disagreements, disgruntlement, and dissatisfaction with the government of the day through peaceful and civilised manner. In addition, the coalition wants to impart to the people the idea that a change of government is possible through the ballot boxes and they should choose the political that best serve their interests.

To achieve the above aim, PR turned its attention to social media. They selected a number of social-media tools to disseminate their message of political awareness to the public, ranging from YouTube and Twitter to blogs and Facebook. These tools were used for different purposes, as illustrated in Table 2.

Table 2: The Usage of Social Media by the People's Coalition

Social Media Tools	Description of Usage
Facebook	Used to provide more information about the individual candidates contesting in the 2013 general election and to disseminate information on campaign events.
YouTube	Used to broadcast speeches made by prominent party leaders throughout the country. The tool was deemed to be the most critical visual channel to educate the public on PR's cause. The tool was also used to introduce the election candidates as they discussed their aspirations and presented their manifestos.

Twitter	Used by the coalition leaders to give quick comments on the issue of the day. Anwar Ibrahim, Rafizi Ramli, and Tony Pua, amongst others, used Twitter extensively and have a large following.
Blogs	Used individually by leaders of PR to disseminate extensive views on the issue of the day. Beyond leaders' blogs, individual bloggers favouring PR also contributed to disseminate views.

To a certain extent, PR's use of social media has proven to be successful. Despite receiving massive mainstream-media coverage, GE13 results showed that the ruling coalition lost seven parliamentary seats and suffered a 2.89 per cent dip in popular votes when compared to their achievement in GE12. In the 2013 general election, the coalition repeated the feat of 2008 by denying the ruling coalition two-thirds majority in the Dewan Rakyat (House of Commons). It also managed to retain two of the richest states in Malaysia, Selangor and Pulau Pinang, retaining Kelantan for twenty-three years running, whilst almost snatching the states of Perak and Terengganu. The coalition also won more parliamentary seats in the Peninsular Malaysia.

However, PR failed to win the general election, as predicted by many political analysts. Although the coalition won the popular votes (52 per cent), it was unable to win more seats in the Dewan Rakyat (parliamentary seats). The seats won by the PR were prominent in the urban parliamentary seats, which correlate to the areas with higher levels of Internet penetration in the country. Its Achilles' heel is in East Malaysia, where the coalition lost heavily. PR's effort to enhance the political awareness did not reach the audience in East Malaysia, compared to West Malaysia. The reasons for its inability to do so will be discussed in detail in the challenges section.

The Use of Social Media to Prevent and Reduce Crime

Another example of the use of social media for social innovation is the Facebook site of the Malaysian Crime Awareness Campaign (MCAC). The site is managed by a small group of dedicated volunteers. The aim of this group is to create awareness of the recent crime wave occurring in Malaysia by consolidating news, experience, video, and blogs on crime. The group hopes that by creating this awareness, the general public can take precautionary measures to avoid being a victim of crime. Consequently, it hopes to make Malaysia a safer place to live.

Most of the postings in MCAC's Facebook site were made by the administration group itself. In addition, almost all the postings were taken from mainstream print and electronic media. This policy ensures that the news have been authenticated before they appear on the site. Contribution from the public comes in the form of feedback and comments to those postings. The site has a strict policy on the kind of postings allowed, which includes banning insults and offensive language or comments that are racial, religious, sexual, or political in nature.

MCAC's initiative has received accolades from many people all over the world, as well as attention from the British Broadcasting Corporation (BBC) and Fox News. However, the extent to which the MCAC's effort has contributed towards enhancing awareness of crime and eventually reducing its occurrence has not been studied. Furthermore, there are many challenges that limit the ability of the group to achieve its aims and objectives. Those challenges will be discussed in the next section.

Challenges in Using Social Media for Social Innovation

Accessibility of Internet

The Malaysian government has put in place plans to provide broadband Internet connections to the whole country. The plan includes providing high-speed broadband Internet to people in urban areas. A cabinet committee on broadband that is headed by the prime minister was formed to spearhead the initiative. To roll out the project, the government has partnered with Telekom Malaysia, because the company has a monopoly on the landlines and is thus able to offer "last-mile" fibre-optic networks, i.e., very high-speed Internet connections to every household (ZD Net 2013).

The results from the Malaysian government's push for broadband have been mixed. Although the government targeted broadband penetration of 15 per cent of the population by 2013, the fixed broadband penetration remains at 8 per cent (Budde.com 2013). Currently, the infrastructure for "last-mile" fibre-optic networks is limited to cities and large towns. It has yet to reach the rural areas of the country. Furthermore, large parts of the East Malaysian states of Sabah and Sarawak are yet to receive broadband Internet.

The limited access to broadband Internet, especially high-speed connections, limits the ability of PR to reach a larger audience. Those without broadband connection will not be able to enjoy the social-media tools such as YouTube that require a fast Internet connection. As a result, this group of people can only rely on news from the mainstream media, where PR does not receive favourable coverage. The lack of Internet access partly explains why PR lost the seats in the rural areas in the 2013 general election.

Trustworthiness of News Delivered through Social Media

There is still a great deal of concern – some of it valid – regarding the verifiability and trustworthiness of news delivered through social media. There is still no mechanism to verify the news delivered through social media, whereby almost everybody is able to post his or her version of the news or share somebody else's version. Although many questioned the trustworthiness of mainstream media in Malaysia, at least it has in place structure and process to edit news before they appear in printed or electronic form.

The group of people most affected by this issue is the older generation. Most of them, especially those living in rural areas, are less exposed to social media, compared to the younger generation or those who live in urban areas where the availability of high-speed Internet access is prevalent. The older generation does not embrace the new and emerging platform of social media as readily as the younger generation. After being exposed to only mainstream media for fifty-six years since independence, the older generation is not that ready to switch allegiance to social media for news. Consequently, even if PR has a strong argument to support the older generation, the message will never reach its intended audience.

One way to enhance the trustworthiness of social media is to control the delivery of news, as practiced by the MCAC. However, this kind of control limits the dynamism of sourcing and delivering news to the people. Dynamism occurs when news come as it happens and from multiple sources. Unfortunately, due to the verification process, only news from certain sources will be included while the rest are ignored. Furthermore, because the verification of news takes time, the social media will not be able to deliver the most up-to-date news to the readers.

The Integration of Social Media into the Overall Strategy

To achieve the maximum potential of IT, the related decision has to be tightly integrated with the organisation's aim and objectives. For example, if one of the objectives was to enhance its customer base, then the organisation has to develop an IT-based system that is able to determine the organisation's current customer base and perhaps propose ways to enlarge it. This kind of practice is also known as "IT governance". The term means that any IT investment and expenditure will provide some value to the organisation.

The same applies to the use of social media by political parties such as PR to enhance political awareness. PR will only gain the optimum value from the use of social media if it is tightly integrated with the coalition's overall strategy. For example, one of the coalition's main strategies was to woo young and new voters who are undecided on whom to support. Since most of these voters are burdened with higher-education loans, PR may create a blog to gain their support for the cause of providing free higher education in the country.

Unfortunately, there is no evidence to suggest that there was a tight integration between the coalition's strategy and its use of social media. Instead, its use of social media can be seen as an afterthought. In other words, the use of social media is not high on PR's agenda. For example, the Facebook pages of the election's candidates were generated very close to the election date. As a result, there was not ample time for the local community to get to know the PR candidates. Since many of them were contesting for the first time in their respective areas, the voters' knowledge of the candidate contributes significantly towards winning or losing that particular seat.

Society's Willingness to Participate in the Initiative

The success of many social innovation programmes relies on the public's willingness to participate in the initiative. Unfortunately, not many in Malaysia want to participate actively and voluntarily. Social-innovation programmes are often moved by a small group of people such as the MCAC administrators. Even the number of people joining as friends is relatively small. There may be various reasons for the larger number of people not getting involved, and one of them could be a "don't bother" attitude.

Anecdotal evidence suggests that people will only get involved voluntarily in crime prevention when they or close family members are victims of crime. This behaviour can be observed in groups organised to support families whose members have certain illnesses or learning disabilities, such as cancer or autism. People joined these groups only when their loved ones were affected by such illness or learning disability. In contrast, others feel less obliged to be involved in such groups. They somehow feel that they and their families are immune to those illnesses.

The success of social innovation such as the MCAC's depends on active participation by the public. When the majority of the public feels that they are immune to being victims of crime, they would not be bothered to get involved in the initiative. Without active public participation, MCAC's information will not reach its intended audience. There will also be less sharing of experience and eventually discussion on how best to avoid being a victim of crime. Consequently, social innovations such as MCAC's will not achieve their aim and objectives.

Possible Legal Ramifications

There are still many unanswered questions about the legal implications of news delivered by individuals on social media or the comments made over that medium. Are the news delivered over social media by individuals considered news or rumours? If they are merely rumours, how should they be treated in a court of law? Should they receive the same treatment as news? Should people receive punishment for perceived over-the-top comments made in social media, especially if they were made against the government? Can a public servant make comments about the government, using this new medium of communication? How should the government of the day behave when facing this new method of self-expression?

The answers to these questions are important to ensure the success and continuity of social innovation through social media. Its success depends heavily on public participation. Without the public's support, the message delivered through this new medium will not reach its intended audience. Imagine if all public servants, some 1 million employees, were banned from making opinions over social media. Would they want to join any social-media activities if they have to watch their backs all the time? It would be a big loss for social innovation if this large group of people was denied the opportunity as well.

There are various opinions about the legality of public servants making comments about the government over social media. Some opinions argue that public servants should not be allowed to do so because it will damage the reputation of the government. It is also perceived as "biting the hands that feed you". Many more argue that public servants should be given the freedom to do so, as long as it is done using their own equipment, outside of working hours and of the department they are a part of. This school of thought believes that public servants are also *the public*. They are also affected by government policies and actions and therefore have the right to voice their grouses in any way possible, including through social media.

Accommodating the new medium of expression requires a new paradigm on the government-citizen relationship. The days are over when the government knows best and the people are expected to submit totally without question. Especially with social media, people want to participate actively in decisions that affect their well-being. Governments today are expected to accommodate criticisms from the public and not be vindictive to the people making them. Many governments, especially in developing countries, are uncomfortable with this new way of governing. Some have gone to the extent of regulating social media, which can deprive this medium the dynamism it currently enjoys. This kind of action may eventually kill social innovation.

Conclusion

The possibilities of social innovation through social media are endless. The success, however, depends on how the new media are used to achieve the aims of social well-being. More studies on how social innovations are made possible through social media are required to better understand the narrative of their success. Hopefully then there will be more theorizing on the topic of social innovation through social media.

References

Alzugaray, S, Mederos, L, and J Sutz (2012). "Building Bridges: Social Inclusion Problems as Research and Innovation Issues". *Review of Policy Research,* 29(6), 776–796.

Choi, S, Park, J-Y, and H W Park (2012). "Using Social Media Data to Explore Communication Processes within South Korean Online Innovation Communities". *Scientometrics,* 90(1), 43–56.

Edwards-Schachter, M E, Matti, C E, and E Alcantara (2012). "Fostering Quality of Life through Social Innovation: A Living Lab Methodology Study Case". *Review of Policy Research,* 29(6), 672–692.

Gladwell, M (2011). "From Innovation to Revolution – Do Social Media Make Protests Possible?" *Foreign Affairs,* 90(2), 153ff.

Jensen, N R (2013). "Action Competence – A New Trial Aimed at Social Innovation in Residential Homes?" *European Journal of Social Work,* 16(1), 120–136.

Oliveira, C and I Breda-Vazquez (2012). "Creativity and Social Innovation: What Can Urban Policies Learn from Sectoral Experiences?" *International Journal of Urban and Regional Research,* 36(3), 522–538.

http://pilihanraya.info/wp-content/uploads/2012/10/WtW.Release.5.pdf. Accessed May 30, 2014.

http://pilihanraya.info/bilikmedia/wtw. Accessed May 30, 2014.

CHAPTER NINE

Appropriating Value from Social Media: Issues and Challenges

Sharan Kaur Garib Singh,[1] **Sharmila Jayasingam,**[1]
Tey Lian Seng,[1] **and Ripan Kumar Saha**[1]

Summary: Social media has received attention from businesses because of its large following of online users. The huge database of users runs into the hundreds of millions, overtaking the populations of some countries. This phenomenal following creates online communities that businesses would like to influence, rather than control. Social media has its own set of rules; if the social-media community senses that they are being controlled commercially, they would "shut out" the user, thus costing repeat and potential customers and causing considerable harm to businesses. In order to appropriate value from social media, organisations have implemented strategies like cross-subsidization, awareness, gratis, social network choices strategies, ensure activity alignment, media plan integration, and access for all. Appropriating value from social media via implementing a string of strategies has

---

[1]   Department of Business Policy and Strategy, Faculty of Business and Accountancy,
       University of Malaya, 50603 Kuala Lumpur, Malaysia.

received very little research attention. Therefore, the aim of this chapter is to identify issues and challenges using the different types of social media and the use of strategies carried out by organisations while appropriating value from social media.

Social Media

The likes of social media was launched around two decades ago with the introduction of Open Diary, a social-networking site for online diary writers, developed by Bruce and Susan Abelson. Social media has transformed substantially since then. The ability of social media – including social-networking sites like Facebook, Twitter, and MySpace (just to name a few) – to capture huge numbers of users has forced businesses to take notice. Conversations about products and services between consumers take place freely and frequently, leaving businesses with less control over the information available about them. Hence, positive and negative business publicity is now easily accessible to consumers through the Internet.

The popularity of social media is evident in both developed and emerging nations. For instance, in Malaysia, as of 11 April 2013, the number of monthly active users of Facebook was 13,369,960. This accounts for 47 per cent of the population (Socialbakers 2013). This figure has almost doubled in two years, as the number of Facebook users in 2010 was 7,317,520 (Burcher 2010). The increased popularity of social-networking sites like Facebook and the like is a worldwide trend. For instance, Facebook had more than 835 million users worldwide (Internet World Stats 2013) in March 2012, up from 175 million active users in January 2009 (Kaplan and Haenlein 2010), an increase of almost fivefold.

This chapter contains theories classifying social media, social media's impact on businesses, and issues and values from appropriating value from social media. The following section attempts to identify a systematic classification of the many types of social-networking sites within social media.

Classification Using Theories on Media Research and Social Processes

A systematic classification of the various types of social media offers a way to distinguish the sites meaningfully, because it provides information on the extent of its impact and influence. Kaplan and Haenlein (2010) have provided a useful categorization of social-media sites, in consonance with two important elements. They derived the two key elements from a bundle of theories grounded in media investigation and social processes. Media research and social practices form the two key elements in the classification of social media. *Media research* comprises social presence and media richness, while *social practices* refers to individual presentation and individual disclosure.

Short, et al. (1976) defined *social presence* as the acoustic, visual, and physical contact achieved between two transmission partners. Based on their findings, social presence is influenced by intimacy (interpersonal vs. mediated) and immediacy (asynchronous vs. synchronous) of the medium. For instance, social presence is less effective for mediated (i.e., telephone/mobile discussion) than interpersonal (i.e., face-to-face conversation) and for asynchronous (i.e., e-mail) than synchronous (i.e., live chat) communication. The extent of social presence determines the influence it has on conversation partners' behaviour; the higher the social presence, the bigger the influence.

According to Daft and Lenger (1986), the theory of media richness is closely associated with social presence, which aims to reduce ambiguity and uncertainty. Media richness differs, and this is determined by the amount of information allowed that is transmitted within a given period. Therefore, some media are more effective than other social media. Hence, the first classification of social media depends on the richness of the medium and the degree of social presence.

The second categorisation of social media is based on the degree of self-disclosure and type of self-presentation. Goffman (1959) explained that self-presentation depicts people's wish to manage the impressions others form of them. In terms of the Internet, self-presentation is observed in the form of a Web page whereby people tend to disclose personal information which coincides with the image of oneself. Thus, Table 1 combines both dimensions that form the classification of social media, as proposed by Kaplan and Haenlein (2010).

Table 1: Classification of Social Media by Social Presence/ Media Richness and Self-Presentation/Self-Disclosure

		Social Presence/Media Richness		
		Low	**Medium**	**High**
Self-Presentation / Self-Disclosure	**High**	Blogs	Social-networking sites (e.g., Facebook)	Virtual social worlds (e.g., Second Life)
	Low	Collaborative Projects (i.e., Wikipedia)	Content Communities (e.g., YouTube)	Virtual game worlds (e.g., World of Warcraft)

Kaplan and Haenlein 2010

Table 1 depicts collaborative projects (e.g., Wikipedia) and blogs to have the lowest score in terms of social presence and media richness because of their simple exchanges and text-based orientation. On a higher level are content communities (e.g., YouTube) and social-networking sites (e.g., Facebook) that allow the sharing of images, videos, and other forms of media in addition to manuscript-based communications. Virtual games and social worlds (e.g., World of Warcraft, Second Life) occupy the highest level, because in a virtual environment, they replicate all dimensions of face-to-face interactions.

In terms of self-presentation and self-disclosure, blogs are on a higher level than collaborative projects, as the latter is focused on specific content domains only. Similarly, content communities are more limiting in their self-disclosure than social-networking sites. Lastly, virtual social worlds have the highest requirement for self-disclosure, even compared to virtual game worlds. The classification of social-media theories leads to the impact of social media on businesses, which is the topic of discussion of the next section.

Impact of Social Media's Qualitative Diversity on Businesses

The impact of social media on businesses is tremendous, and this phenomenon is growing ever more complex because of its qualitative diversity. Social media's diversity permeates in three ways. First, the speed at which it has impacted businesses is a force to be reckoned with. Second, social media's effects are seen affecting business in its entire activity, from product development to customer support. Third, firms are forced to engage in social media if their customers are already involved in it.

Social media has received attention from businesses because of its large following of online users. The huge database of online users runs into the hundreds of millions, overtaking the populations of some countries. This phenomenal following of users creates online communities that businesses would like to influence, rather than control. Social media have some sets of rules. If the social-media community senses that they are being controlled commercially, they tend to "shut out" the user, thus costing repeat and potential customers, causing considerable harm to businesses.

The ability of social media to provide word-of-mouth marketing at scale garners a huge impact on sales and marketing for business-to-business (B2B) and business-to-customer (B2C) firms. Customers now become marketing agents for firms when they influence their friends, family, and colleagues within their social network toward certain products or services. Alternatively, they hinder sales when they provide bad reviews of products or services. According to Argenti (2011), firms find themselves embracing social media as a necessity, rather than an option for business strategy. Moreover, social networking is shifting the way public relations are practiced today (Wright and Hinson 2012). Compared to a few years ago, firms today are more likely to dedicate resources to social media and involve in dialogue with stakeholders (Burson and Marsteller 2011).

Social media has huge cost implications for businesses as well. Marketing costs are decreased significantly with social media, as firms use social media to promote online. This is seen happening amongst some businesses in Malaysia. For example, Digi, a mobile operator in Malaysia, used mostly Facebook and Twitter to create a competition by allowing community members to attach creative videos on the site. With this contest, Digi was able to spread the word and conversations with the community.

The social-networking bandwagon now contains many big and small firms that maintain Facebook pages and groups. One company that has a huge following on their Facebook pages is AirAsia, which promotes some aspect of their service via twenty different Facebook pages and groups. Its fan bases of approximately two hundred thousand (Yeoh 2010) leads all other airlines. As a result, the AirAsia's blog is graded the world's second-most-popular blog site by an airline, whilst its CEO Tony Fernandez's blog is also the most popular by a corporate leader in Malaysia. AirAsia's active investment of time and effort to engage social networkers is seen as beneficial, as the airline gains huge mileage in terms of addressing customer feedback of their travel experience. This also creates some form of trust and reliance, especially when users gain real-time information about airport conditions and their flight details. In return, AirAsia rewards users by giving discounts to their social-network fans.

The following section discusses at length the issues and challenges faced by businesses in appropriating value from social media.

Appropriating Value from Social Media: Issues and Challenges

The last twenty years have brought significant changes, making organisational boundaries more fluid and dynamic in response to the growing swiftness of social media. We aspire to identify the generic strategy of social media by re-examining the construct of co-specialization and considering additional strategies to generate an appropriate value from social media. This allows us to create an innovative set of predictions, which might assist in navigating the increasingly complex and dynamic competitive landscape in the age of local and global competition faced by companies.

Appropriating Value through the Use of Different Types of Social Media

Collaborative Projects

Collaborative projects allow joint collaboration of simultaneous content creation by numerous users. This produces the most democratic display of user-generated content (UGC). Wikis and social-bookmarking applications are two types of collaborative projects. Text-based content in wikis can be added, removed, and changed, while social-bookmarking applications permit group-based users to compile and rate content. Wikipedia is an example of a wiki, which is an online encyclopaedia that is accessible in 230 different languages. Delicious, a social-bookmarking application, permits users to store and share Web bookmarks.

According to Fama (1970), the basic idea behind collaborative projects is to produce better results collectively. Individual accomplishments may not be as significant as joint attempts by more than one user. From a business point of view, companies must realise that the trend of collaborative projects is becoming the key source of information for many customers. Thus, even though all written material on Wikipedia may not actually be true, it is considered to be true for a growing number of Internet users. This can be particularly important in terms of corporate crises. For instance, while online book retailer Amazon.com began testing the idea of dynamic pricing, comments appeared immediately, declaring that such a practice is unfair under the Wikipedia entry on "time-based pricing". However, collaborative projects also provide a number of unique opportunities for companies. For example, mobile telephone manufacturer Nokia used internal wikis to update employees on the status of projects and trade ideas that are used by 20 per cent of their sixty-eight thousand employees. Similarly, software company Adobe Systems in the United States maintains a list of bookmarks to company-associated websites and conversations on Delicious.

Blogs

Blogs symbolise the oldest form of social media, a special type of websites that normally show date-stamped entries in reverse sequential order (OECD 2007). A blog is the social-media version of a personal Web page and can come in a huge number of variations, from describing the author's life in the form of personal diaries to summaries of all kinds of information in one particular content area. Generally, blogs are maintained by an individual, but it enables interaction with other people by adding comments. Text-based blogs are still the most common, due to their historical roots. However, blogs have also started to take different media formats. For instance, San Francisco-based Justin.tv allows users to generate their own television channels, where they can publish images from their webcam in real time to the whole world.

To update employees, customers, and shareholders about their important developments, many companies are currently using blogs. CEO of Sun Microsystems, Jonathan Schwartz, has a personal blog to improve the transparency of his company. Nevertheless, as is the case with collaborative projects, blogs are not risk-free. These risks usually occur in two situations. First, according to Ward and Ostrom (2006), customers who are displeased or disappointed with the offerings of the company may decide to make virtual complaints by creating protest websites or blogs, thus exposing harmful information online. Second, when companies inspire their employees to actively participate in the blogs, they may have to live with the consequences of staff writing negative comments about the company. For instance, Microsoft's former "technical evangelist", Robert Scoble, had a propensity to criticise the products of his employer before leaving the Redmond-based software company in 2006.

Content Communities

The main purpose of online content communities is to share media content amongst users. The content community is available for a wide range of media types, including text (e.g., BookCrossing, over 130 countries with more than 700,000 people sharing books); photos (e.g., Flickr); videos (e.g., YouTube); and PowerPoint presentations (e.g., Slideshare). The content community's users are not required to create an individual profile page; however, if they do, it generally only comprises basic information, like the date they joined the society and the number of videos shared.

From a business standpoint, content communities carry the threat of being used as platforms for sharing copyright-protected materials. While the main content communities have introduced rules to prevent and eliminate such illegal content, it is very tough to prevent popular videos – such as recent episodes of TV dramas – from being uploaded to YouTube only hours after they have been aired. On the positive side, the immense popularity of content communities garners huge interest from many companies, making it easy to believe that YouTube serves over 100 million videos per day.

In 2007, Procter and Gamble organised a competition for its over-the-counter drug Pepto-Bismol, which has enticed users to upload to YouTube one-minute videos of themselves singing about the diseases that can be treated by Pepto-Bismol. In the same vein, kitchen equipment manufacturer Blendtec became famous as millions of people watched their "Will it blend?" videos. Other companies, such as Cisco and Google, depend on online communities to share recruiting videos and also keynote speeches and press notices with their employees and investors.

Social-Networking Sites

Social-networking sites allow users to connect to each other by creating personal profiles, inviting friends and colleagues to gain access to those profiles, and sending e-mails and instant messages between each other. This personal profile has all kinds of information, including images, videos, audio records, and blogs. According to Wikipedia, the biggest social-networking sites are US-based Facebook (originally founded by Mark Zuckerberg to stay in touch with his fellow students from Harvard University) and MySpace (with 1,500 employees and more than 250 million registered users). Thus, social networking sites are highly popular, especially amongst young Internet users.

Some companies have been using social-networking sites to create brand communities, whilst others use social-networking sites for marketing research (Kozinets 2002; Muniz and O'Guinn 2001). For the promotion of the film, *Fred Claus,* Warner Brothers created a Facebook profile where visitors can watch trailers, play games, and download graphics. Similarly, the Adidas community on MySpace allows visitors to access reviews of products and information on professional soccer players who play using Adidas's shoes. Some innovative companies use Facebook as a distribution channel, like American florist 1-800-Flowers. com. This florist offers users "virtual bouquets" to be sent to their friends or loved ones, and with a click of the mouse, users are directly transferred to the company's website, where they can send real flowers.

Another social-media site that is gaining traction rapidly is Instagram, a photo-sharing site that was developed in 2010 and has been recently acquired by Facebook for US $1 billion. It has 130 million users (Good 2013) with an average monthly audience of 32 million, and it is said to be the fastest-growing site, with a 66 percent increase in 2013 (Knibbs 2013). In addition to photo sharing, Instagram also has video capability, which it launched in June 2013. Instagram's photo and video features provide companies in both B2B and B2C realms, giving companies an opportunity to build a whole new visual identity. This helps develop deeper connections between customers, as well as potential customers and these companies (Good 2013). For example, Nike has used a video on Instagram to promote their new campaign, whilst GE's Instagram account has inspiring pictures of its otherwise "dull and dry" industrial products (Good 2013).

Virtual Game Worlds

Virtual worlds are platforms which provide opportunities for users to portray themselves as avatars in a three-dimensional environment. In virtual worlds, users, as avatars, can interact with other avatars as they would in real life. In this case, virtual worlds depict the highest form of social media, as its combination of social presence and media richness surpasses all preceding applications discussed thus far.

There are two types of virtual worlds. The first is the virtual game world. Virtual game world users are required to adhere to strict rules in the context of a massive multiplayer online role-playing game (MMORPG). Virtual worlds' application has grown in popularity in recent years. Standard gaming consoles – including Microsoft's Xbox and Sony's PlayStation – are now allowing users to play simultaneously with multitudes of players around the world. Examples of virtual game worlds include World of Warcraft and EverQuest. World of Warcraft has approximately 8.5 million users who explore the virtual world of

Azeroth in search of treasure while fighting monsters. Users can take many forms, such as human beings, dwarves, orcs, or night elves.

Sony's EverQuest comprises sixteen different races of players (e.g., mages, priests) who travel the fantasy world of Norrath. The extent of self-presentation and self-disclosure are often limited by the rules of such games. Nevertheless, users' characters, be it a dragon or a dwarf, tend to resemble their real-life personality. This is common with users who spend long hours with these applications. A plus factor for companies with virtual worlds is that their popularity can be used in conventional communication programmes. For example, the giant Japanese automotive company Toyota used images and mechanics from the World of Warcraft application in its Tundra advertisement.

Virtual Social Worlds

Virtual social worlds, often called the second group of virtual worlds, allow users to select their behaviour more liberally and live a virtual life as their real life. Similar to virtual game worlds, virtual social world users appear in the form of avatars and interact in a virtual environment in three dimensions; however, virtual social world users are free to interact without any restrictions. According to Haenlein and Kaplan (2009), virtual social worlds allow an unlimited variety of self-presentation strategies and with increased usage intensity and consumption experience, users' behaviour more and more closely reflects the behaviour observed in the real-life context.

The most popular virtual social world is the Second Life application by the San Francisco-based company Linden Research, Inc. In addition to doing all that is possible in real life (such as talking to other avatars, running, enjoying the virtual sunshine), content can also be created by users of Second Life. For instance, users can design furniture and clothes. Interestingly, users can use a virtual currency traded against the US dollar on the Second Life Exchange to sell their designs to others in exchange for Linden dollars. A number of users are so good at it that the virtual money earned complements their real-life income. Kaplan and Haenlein (2009) gave examples of the various opportunities for businesses that virtual social worlds offer, such as marketing, human-resource management, and internal process management.

Appropriating Value from Social Media through Selected Strategy Implementation

The implementation of various strategies by firms in gaining value from social media closely reflects the type of benefits firms plan to accrue. Specifically, the following discusses three types of strategies implemented by firms in order to garner as much as possible from social media.

Cross-Subsidisation

The matching of one product to compensate the cost of another product refers to product cross-subsidisation. This is similar to the "razor and blade" strategy, whereby the razor is sold cheaply, whilst the blade is pricy and is the way sellers make their margins. Gillette initially adopted this, which is a similar strategy to printer manufacturers and video-game companies (Jones and Hill 2010). The printers and consoles are sold relatively cheaply, but the ink and games, with repeat sales, are priced high for higher margins.

The other type of cross-subsidisation is customer (market) cross-subsidisation, the practice of charging higher prices to one group of customers (markets), in order to subsidise lower prices for another group of customers (markets). In market cross-subsidisation, people can easily discover the price difference between different markets through advertisements in the social network. They will perceive firms as pursuing price discrimination, and their benefit has been exploited. The reputation of the firms will inevitably be affected. In this situation, firms look for a way to control the advertisements that can only reach certain group of consumers (markets). In other words, firms need to decide which social network is most suitable as the medium to appropriate value from the strategy.

Gratis

Gratis is a new product that is given out to customers for free, in the hope of getting feedback to improve the quality of the product. In general, people who are involved enjoy interacting and making contributions. For instance, LEGO has invited customers to provide feedback on new designs and products, and the gift would be LEGO's formal recognition. For the user, acceptance of the firm to build on their ideas and design into the final product is recognition that is well received by customers.

The beauty of a social network is that it can reach a vast audience within a short period of time. If firms pursue this strategy through social networking, they need to address the quantity of free products and feedback they need to give and receive, because the free participation may substitute for some other activity that will have cost implications. For instance, firms need to increase the number of customer-service staff to give out the free products and monitor customer feedback across geographical regions and time zones.

Awareness

A variety of social media-based activities achieve the goal of increasing awareness, whether of the firm (by the customer), the customer (by the firm), or peers (by other customers). Stakeholders may become aware of a new product, service, or event or of an existing or potential problem. Awareness may be accomplished directly (by express contact with one stakeholder by another), or indirectly (via monitoring customer activity). Within the process of community-building, awareness is a first step for firms to take toward developing customer loyalty. In the context of one customer making another contact aware of the products, services, etc., we see online word-of-mouth effects occur. When firms use social media to make customers aware of new products or services, we can understand this as traditional online marketing.

From the consumer's viewpoint, it is useful to employ social media as an expedient route for marketing and making firms aware of product flaws; this accomplishes customer service, especially benefitting the firm (and other customers) in cases where it is necessary to act quickly to defuse a potential large-scale problem. Through the mechanism of monitoring customer-to-customer interactions, firms are also able to make themselves aware of consumer dissatisfaction and adverse events, subsequently enabling them to take appropriate action anticipatorily.

Weak Signals

As social media constantly flood us with information, it is easy to miss out snippets of valuable information termed as "weak signals" by Harryson, Metayer, and Sarrazin (2014). These snippets of information are not streams of information, but they are powerful enough to garner top-management attention. Such information prompts businesses to take the next step in probing further the implications it can have on meeting customer needs, thus overtaking competitors in spotting potential industry and market disruptions. Weak signals are spotted during data analyses; at other times, weak signals are picked up by employees who use methods more akin to art than science. These are then subjected to further research or number-crunching, to figure out the anomalies or hypotheses they are seeing.

Harryson, et al. (2014) suggest engaging senior executives in social-media sources that provide weak signals. For example, one sensitive social listener who happens to be a senior executive of a global manufacturer commissioned research to substantiate a hunch after spotting a customer's recent post about the company's high-quality and low-priced products. The research result showed the low price to be an anomaly, but the quality of the product was widely held. This induced the manufacturer to concentrate marketing efforts in emphasising its quality to grow market share by further differentiating itself from the competitors.

In another example, the missing information on childcare via keyword searches on social media compelled a global advertising company (which was investigating childcare services for a client) to follow subtle conversations of parents on social media, using semantic clues. This anthropological view of childcare produced vital information about the availability of different services in individual markets, the specific service levels sought by parents, the prices parents were willing to pay, the existing company-sponsored childcare options, the strength of local providers, and potential ambassadors in various communities for a new service. This exercise was extensive, but it didn't involve number-crunching; instead it required the analysts to piece together snippets of information from various social-media sources. As a result, the advertising company was able to delineate the gap in childcare services (Harryson, et al. 2014).

From the four strategies of cross-subsidisation, gratis, awareness, and weak signals, firms must also decide which of the many social media, in particular social networks, would be most cost-effective to indulge in. Hence, the next section explains the choice of social network used by firms to garner huge benefits.

Social Network Choices Strategies

Choosing Carefully

A strategic plan is a firm's game plan (David 2012). Firms need to know how to play the game, once they have decided which game to play. In order to win the game, an additional "battlefield" exists, where firms include social networks with conventional media to attract more customers.

There are thousands of social networks, and new ones are emerging in the market every day. Whether the social network is active or not, it has its own features and target groups. Choosing the right social network amongst the many depends on the target market. Thus, it is impossible for firms to participate in them all.

As mentioned above, there are thousands of social networks in the market, and how to identify the right one may be another issue firms face. Firms not only need to come up with some criteria to select the right social network, but they also need to know where to gather those data. As a result, firms need to spend plenty of time and manpower to choose the right social network to serve their purpose. For instance, an alternative-energy-drink manufacturer that provides health drinks may want to target a content community that lives by a healthy living code.

Hence, choosing the right social network to effectively and efficiently exploit the market opportunities has become one of the challenges to firms.

Pick or Make Your Own

"Build your own site or buy one" would be the theme of this strategy. Instead of reinventing the wheel, it is recommended that firms use a presented social-media site and take advantage of its existing database of users.

Worst of all, if there is no "right" social network available in the market to serve the firm's purpose, firms have no other choice but to develop the network on their own. If firms have the expertise in developing the network, they may only need to bear the cost and spend some time to build the network. If firms do not have the capability to develop their own network, it will be a high risk for them to be involved in the project. Thus, firms may be in a dilemma between choosing to use the existing social network and developing the new network to serve their firm.

Activity Alignment

Activity alignment of social media focuses on the effectiveness of achieving a firm's objectives. Firms cannot depend solely on one social medium to serve a particular purpose; therefore, being involved in several for varied purposes gives firms an advantage, as various types of social media have various types of features. However, this requires firms to align different activities based on the social medium's features. For instance, using Facebook, firms can publish and post photos, videos, and many more messages than other media such as Twitter. Firms might decide to use several social media to garner the highest reach of users, and this will be useful if all activities in these varying sites are aligned. In other words, the message that the firm sends out is the same.

Media Plan Integration

Media plan integration of social media focuses on efficiencies. If a video featuring the firm's product becomes hugely successful on social media, it is worth airing the same video on traditional media such as television. For the consumer, it reinforces the corporate image of the company, hence, as with alignment of differing social media, integration of media is key.

Strength

According to Gilbert (2009), the amount of time, the emotional intensity, the intimacy, and the reciprocal services are jointly combined to form tie strength. Ties are either strong or weak. Strong ties are ties with the people we really trust, people whose social loops tightly overlap with our own. In contrast, acquaintances represent weak ties. Weak ties can be described as access to novel information that is not circulated in the closely knit social circle of strong ties.

Gilbert (2009) discovered that social media could forecast tie strength, whereby numerous opportunities exist to apply tie-strength modelling in social media, which is regarded as privacy controls. Once users construct privacy choices, a system could make knowledgeable estimates about which friends fall into trusted and untrusted categories. This may be also based on types of media. For example, more sensitive media like photos require greater tie strengths. There are two main advantages – it changes with time and sets smart defaults for users setting access levels for friends. Recently, social media has developed the ability to suggest new friends to users. Yet, sometimes a user chooses not to be a friend of someone, with good reason. For example, one doesn't call someone a friend just because that someone is a strong tie to one's own strong tie. A system that knows tie strength may keep away from strain by navigating clear of these fragile circumstances.

Although social media brings huge benefits to firms, these firms have been faced with many challenges.

Issues in Social Media

Legal Issues

Social media can pose a variety of potential legal problems for those who choose to exploit the technology. One of the problems associated with the development of social media that concerns management and administrators is what action to take when confronted with damaging information to customers or others. The volume of information coming from a customer base makes it nearly impossible to check all of the contents. A question that many firms' leaders have is, "How do I respond if a specific posting, be it offensive or threatening, is called to my attention?"

Reputation Issues

Firms are threatened in several ways when it comes to the possibility or danger of losing their reputation. According to Jenny (2003), the loss of reputation affects competitiveness, local and international positioning, customer trust and loyalty, supplier trust and loyalty, media relations, legitimacy of operations, and license to exist.

Social media fuels new hopes or beliefs about firms, to which firms should pay attention. Expectations are created regarding ethical business practices and the transparency of operations. Moreover, the users of social media spread their views about which area or issues firms should give more attention in the future. There are several types of social media sites that question the responsibilities and administration of the firms, demand transparency, and reveal corporate irresponsibility (Aula, 2010). For example, the multi-lingual Business & Human Rights Resource Centre (2014) website highlight business practices that violate human rights. Even the actions of non-governmental organisations (NGOs) are not left without scrutiny by social media users. NGOMONITOR (2014) provides a platform for social media users to report unscrupulous behaviours and actions of NGOs throughout the world.

On the other hand, reputational risk could be a result of the firm's own communication activities, including their response to claims presented in the social media. Firms have been caught amending the facts in online encyclopaedias, such as Wikipedia, for their own interests, and also maintaining fake company blogs (or "flogs"). American television network Fox edited its entry in Wikipedia more than a hundred times, while Wal-Mart was responsible for establishing a popular consumer travel blog. Such measures taken by firms are known as "distorted reality", as information is displayed to place the firm in a positive light, but when revealed, it harms the firm.

The management of strategic reputation of the firm must focus on ethics, rather than short-term interests. With the existence of social media, firms should have a clear guideline for how to behave in order to live up to expectations and how to communicate a business objective. For instance, if firms pay so-called customers to influence an online discussion or recommend a company's products in social media, it raises a lot of questions about the integrity and values of managers behind the company and also risks the company's reputation. In social media, a firm cannot just *look* good; it has to *be* good.

Ethical Issues

The use of social media ranges from having personal communication with friends and family to professional communication with colleagues, suppliers, and clients. Occasionally, information concerning customers, suppliers, and competitors overlaps, and is inseparable in the social-media context (Boyd 2007). Thus, it is no surprise that an endless web of controversies seems to emerge in social-media usage when private and public lives are combined. Issues of the ethical use of social media take centre stage. This has given rise to research topics and media attention that have caused the increased identification and comprehension of the base ethical issues of social-media usage.

The emergence of ethical issues in social media has created a dilemma, because the original design of social media was for social communications, which traditionally, most adults have considered a private and protected space. Fortunately or unfortunately, those communications are subject to public scrutiny, as they are exposed to the whole world. Under the public eye, the focal individual has no control over the way in which the communications are used, thus giving rise to ethical debates that spiral into several ethical questions prompting Cain, et al. (2010) to categorise those ethical questions according to five primary criteria:

(1) the viewer of social-media information;
(2) access to information from social media;

(3) the reason for using social-media information;

(4) the criteria for making judgments about information in social media; and

(5) the nature of "relationships" in social media.

A brief explanation of each of the five criteria follows.

(1) The Viewer of Social-Media Information

A basic ethical question is, "Can it be acceptable for someone outside a person's social network to view the individual's social-media information?" Even though one is of the opinion that information posted is considered "public", there is still an ethical question of whether that "public" is an "open public". Most of the conversations of firms happening through social media are aimed at a select group of consumers or potential consumers. Some argue that a person's privacy is violated when someone outside the planned audience views his or her social media.

(2) Access to Information from Social Media

An important ethical issue pertains to the purpose of someone who becomes privy to the social-media information of another. It is one thing for a person to see another individual's social-media information, especially when the former has been given access to it. Conversely, if the information is presented by a third party like a colleague, supplier, or competitor for a prize, honour, or employment, then it is a different matter to access that information. Hence, a number of people believe that regardless of how information is exposed, information freely and voluntarily provided to the public is open for scrutiny.

(3) The Reason for Using Social-Media Information

Using online social-media information other than for social reasons raises an ethical issue. Many people are not comfortable viewing information for purposes of anything except social communication, as they are of the view that these applications were designed for socialising. The central issue arising out of this elicits the following question: is it correct to use social media to make decisions related to the selection of products or any other decisions of a non-social nature?

A central and frequent discussion topic pertains to using social-media information for decisions on employment and securing a contract or project. It could be argued that this information may be more revealing than what is discoverable during job applications and interviews. This information could lead to better decisions made by admissions committees about candidates who present similar scores or ratings. Individuals and companies who are not cautious with the information they publish online or who are not adequately industrious in protecting access to it may not have the appropriate skills or judgment necessary to work in a professional environment.

(4) The Criteria for Making Judgments about Information in Social Media

Information contained in personal social profiles becomes a complex task when it is used for interpreting character, professionalism, and other individuals' or firms' characteristics. The information posted on social media may or may not reflect the true picture of the personas of individuals or the goings-on of firms.

(5) The Nature of "Relationships" in Social Media

The last category of ethical issues in social media pertains to the character of social-networking relationships. Employees becoming Facebook friends or liking competitors with advertisement of competing firms is a bit of a contentious issue. Cain (2009) raised the issue about harm that comes to employees when they are aware of company information from competitor "friends" who are involved in illegal acts or who commit e-professionalism transgressions. While there may be advantages in dealing with social media, overexposure to their personal life may lead to negative results for both. Therefore, every employee should at least think about the implications of interacting with rivals via social media.

Conclusion

The ability of social media – which comprises social-networking sites like Twitter, Facebook, Instagram, and MySpace (to name just a few) – to capture huge users has forced businesses to take notice. Social media has a tremendous impact on businesses today because conversations about products and services between consumers take place freely and frequently, leaving businesses with less control over the information available about them. Positive and negative business publicity are now easily accessible to consumers through the Internet.

The many different types of social media have prompted us to highlight the categorization of social media based on media research theory and social processes theory. This systematic classification offers a way to distinguish the sites meaningfully, because it provides information on the extent of social media's impact and influence, thus making it easier to understand the different types of social media. In addition, we have also identified a list of strategies used by businesses to appropriate value from social media. These strategies include cross-subsidisation, gratis, awareness, weak signals, social network choices strategies, ensure activity alignment, media plan integration, and access for all. These allow us to create an innovative set of predictions which might help navigate the ever more complex and dynamic competitive landscape faced by firms in the era of international and global business competition.

Issues and challenges in terms of garnering value from social media have also been discussed. The main issue is the influence on businesses when users impart bad publicity regarding products or services used, creating an adverse impact on the bottom line. Moreover, online exchanges that take place between friends may lead to revealing of sensitive information that could be accessible to friends of friends that work for competitors, thus leading to legal as well as ethical implications. Nevertheless, the value and benefits appropriated from social media significantly outweigh the negative impact it has, which forces businesses to take notice of it. In sum, social media will be part of business strategy for a long time to come.

References

Argenti, P (2011). "Digital Strategies for Powerful Corporate Communications". Retrieved 4 July 2011 from the *European Financial Review* at *http://www.europeanfinancialreview.com/?p=2581*.

Aula, P (2010). "Social Media, Reputation Risk and Ambient Publicity Management". *Strategy & Leadership*, Vol. 38(6), 43-50.

Boyd, D (2007). "Social Network Sites: Public, Private, or What?" *The Knowledge Tree*. 13 (May) 28.

Burcher, N (2010). "Facebook Usage Statistics by Country – July 2010 Compared to July 2009 and July 2008". Retrieved 11 April 2013 from *http://www.nickburcher.com/2010/07/facebook-usage-statistics-bycountry.html*.

Burson and Marsteller (2011). "Fortune Global 100 Social Media Study". Retrieved from *http://www.bursonmarsteller.com/Innovation_and_insights/blogs_and_podcast.s/BM_Blog/Lists/Posts/Post.aspx?List=75c7a224-05a3-4f25-9ce52a90a7c0c761&ID=254*.

Business & Human Rights Resource Centre (2014). Retrieved 24 July 2014 from http://business-humanrights.org/en.

Cain, J and F Romanelli (2009). "E-professionalism: A New Paradigm for a Digital Age", *Currents Pharm Teach Learn*, Vol. 1(2), 66–70.

Cain, J and L Joseph (2010). "Legal and Ethical Issues Regarding Social Media and Pharmacy Education". *American Journal of Pharmaceutical Education,* Vol. 74(10) 184.

Daft, R L and R H Lengel (1986). "Organizational Information Requirements, Media Richness, and Structural Design". *Management Science,* Vol. 32(5), 554–571.

David, F R (2012). *Strategic Management: Concepts and Cases,* 14th Edition. Old Tappan, New Jersey: Prentice-Hall International.

Fama, E F (1970). "Efficient Capital Markets: A Review of Theory and Empirical Work." *Journal of Finance*, Vol. 25(2), 383–417.

Gilbert, E and Karahalios, K. (2009). *Predicting Tie Strength with Social Media*. Retrieved 24 July 2014 from https://www.cs.purdue.edu/homes/aliaga/cs197-10/papers/predicting-tie-strength.pdf.

Goffman, E (1959). *The Presentation of Self in Everyday Life*. New York: Doubleday Anchor Books.

Good, S (2013). "What's All the Buzz about Instagram – and How Should I Use It?" Retrieved 2 April 2014 from *https://savvypanda. com/blog/beginner-level/how-to-use-instagram.html*.

Haenlein, M and A M Kaplan (2009). "Flagship Brand Stores within Virtual Worlds: The Impact of Virtual Store Exposure on Real-Life Brand Attitudes and Purchase Intent". *Rechercheet Applications en Marketing*, Vol. 24(3) 57–81.

Harryson, M, Metayer, E, and H Sarrazin (2014). "The Strength of 'Weak Signals'". Retrieved 4 April 2014 from *http://www.mckinsey.com/ insights/high_tech_telecoms_internet/the_strength_of_weak_signals*.

Internet World Stats (2013). "Facebook Users in the World". Retrieved 11 April 2013 from *http://www.internetworldstats.com/facebook.htm*.

Jones, G R and C W L Hill (2010). *Theory of Strategic Management with Cases*, 9th Edition. International Edition, Singapore: South-Western Cengage Learning.

Kaplan, A M and M Haenlein (2009). "Consumer Use and Business Potential of Virtual Worlds: The Case of Second Life". *The International Journal on Media Management*, Vol. 11(3) 93–101.

_____ (2009). "Consumers, Companies, and Virtual Social Worlds: A Qualitative Analysis of Second Life". *Advances in Consumer Research,* Vol. 36(1), 873–874.

_____ (2009). "The Fairyland of Second Life: About Virtual Social Worlds and How to Use Them". *Business Horizons,* Vol. 52(6), 563–572.

_____ (2010). "Users of the World, Unite! The Challenges and Opportunities of Social Media". *Business Horizons,* Vol. 53, 59–68.

Knibbs, K (2013). "Nielsen Research Finds that When it Comes to Mobile, Instagram Beats Twitter". Retrieved 2 April 2014 from *http://www.digitaltrends.com/social-media/mobile-instagram-beats-twitter/#!CtQYB*.

Kozinets, R V (2002). "The Field Behind the Screen: Using Netnography for Marketing Research in Online Communities". *Journal of Marketing Research*, Vol. 39(1), 61–72.

Muniz, A M and T C O'Guinn (2001). "Brand Community". *Journal of Consumer Research*, Vol. 27(4), 412–432.

NGOMONITOR (2014). Retrieved 24 July 2014 from http://www.ngo-monitor.org/index.php.

Rayner, J (2003). *Managing Reputational Risk: Curbing Threats, Leveraging Opportunities.* Chichester, UK: John Wiley and Sons.

Short, J, Williams, E, and B Christie (1976). *The Social Psychology of Telecommunications.* Hoboken, NJ: John Wiley and Sons, Ltd.

Socialbakers (2013). Malaysia Facebook statistics. Retrieved 11 April 2013 from *http://www.socialbakers.com/facebook-statistics/malaysia*.

Ward, J C, and A L Ostrom (2006). "Complaining to the Masses: The Role of Protest Framing in Customer-Created Complaint Web Sites". *Journal of Consumer Research,* Vol. 33(2), 220–230.

Wright, D and M Hinson (2012). *A Four-Year Longitudinal Analysis Measuring Social and Emerging Use in Public Relations Practice.* Paper presented at the International Public Relations Research Conference, Miami, Fla.

Yeoh, S. H. (2010). *http://www.tnooz.com/2010/04/07/news/air-asia-claims-social-media-victory-admits-huge-resources-needed-to-manage/.*

CHAPTER TEN

Challenges Facing Modelling the Spread of Infectious Diseases in the Community and Congregate Settings

Noor Azina Ismail[1], Herlianna Naning1, Ofosuhene O. Apenteng1, Adeeba Kamaruzzaman1, and Haider A. A. Al-Darraji[2]

Summary: In trying to project the spread of infectious diseases in the general population and in closed settings, researchers face many challenges. Such challenges might include difficulties in obtaining reliable empiric data and choosing the appropriate model. Ethical issues are common and may present as a major obstacle when conducting research studies, particularly in marginalised populations. Whilst most research trials, particularly those related to infectious diseases, are designed to evaluate incidence rates in the population of interest, in comparison to a control group, ethical obligations would call for an equal intervention package for both research groups, to protect the

---

[1]   Department of Applied Statistics, Faculty of Economics and Administration, University of Malaya, 50603 Kuala Lumpur, Malaysia.
[2]   Centre of Excellence for Research in AIDS (CERIA), University of Malaya, 50603 Kuala Lumpur, Malaysia.

control group. In this chapter, we discuss these challenges in addition to the logistical and structural barriers and research bias faced while conducting such trials.

Introduction

The spread of infectious diseases is a major health concern in many parts of the world. Another problem that is beginning to attract more attention is co-morbidities, where multiple pathogen species infect a human body. Co-infection is now considered much more commonplace than was previously perceived. It leads to interaction effects between the pathogens that may alter previously understood patterns of the spread of disease. Furthermore, co-infection complicates clinical care and morbidity and mortality; in the prison context, the problem is even worse. This chapter intends to analyse the patterns of co-infection amongst diseases that reflects geographical (spatial) distributions within communities, towns, districts, cities, regions, and the whole country. The aim of this study is to extend our knowledge of how a mathematical model can be used to supplement the model of co-infection involving HIV and other associated diseases, as well as to identify appropriate strategies for constructing mathematical models that best fit the real-world data. These models may then be useful for extracting parameter values for exposure, susceptibility, and infection that can be used in future preventative strategies. Co-infection infection, morbidity, and transmission patterns will be compared.

Social networking has become one of the biggest networks for different people to interact with different numbers of individuals and with some individuals more than others and this affects impact of individual's behaviors in many ways, depending on the state of the existing network and the goal of the intervention. In order for any disease to spread there is contact between the infected individual and susceptible individual. In this case the HIV individual play the pivotal role to network that could lead the spread of the disease. For instance, HIV prevention would be used to address the issues and challenges of how social network is used public health preventive methods. Some of these social network issues and challenges of individual will discuss how tuberculosis (TB) amongst dependent prison inmates contributes the spread of the disease.

In addition, this study will also model the spread of tuberculosis (TB) amongst inmates in a correctional facility in Malaysia. TB prevalence in correctional facilities is estimated to be up to one hundred times higher, compared to the general population (World Health Organisation 2000). A cohort study in a Malaysian prison reported a very high (16.7 per cent) prevalence of active TB amongst the HIV-infected inmates (Al-Darraji et al. 2012). The high rates of TB in correctional facilities are likely attributed to the higher risk of TB amongst the incarcerated population with prevalent alcohol and drug users, HIV infection, history of incarceration, homelessness, and illegal immigrants with a history of contact in a high-TB-prevalence environment (Moller et al. 2009).

Other factors, such as poor ventilation, overcrowding, and high turnover of inmates facilitate the rapid reactivation of latent TB infection (LTBI). LTBI is recognised as the most prevalent infection amongst inmates in correctional facilities (Baussano et al. 2010). Evidence found that nearly 70 per cent of inmates in Singapore had LTBI (Al-Darraji et al. 2012), while a study by Baussano et al (2010) estimated that for every LTBI incidence in the general population, there are twenty-six cases of LTBI amongst the inmate population.

To complicate the matter, inmates who are HIV-infected are in greater risk of getting TB, as evidence shows that HIV-infected populations have more than a twentyfold increased risk of active TB than those without HIV (Pawlowski et al. 2012). Moreover, immuno-suppressed individuals have a 5 to 8 per cent annual risk of developing active TB and a 30 per cent lifetime risk, as compared to a healthy person, with only a 10 per cent lifetime risk (Selwyn et al. 1989). The WHO reported that one in four HIV-related deaths was caused by TB and some 430,000 people died of HIV-associated TB in 2011 (World Health Organization 2012). The facility staff members who are in close contact with inmates daily expose their families to the threat of TB infection, which could eventually spread to the community (The *PLoS Medicine* Editors, 2010).

This chapter describes various research issues and challenges in modelling co-infection when population characteristics or their possible migration routes are taken into account. Different sets of problems and challenges in conducting such a study in a closed setting will also be discussed.

Importance of the Topic

There has been longstanding interest on how to model population movements in order to find optimal control strategies for one particular disease. In the absence of vaccines and treatments, the only method to stop disease from spreading is to control population movements. Human mobility is one of the causes of the geographical spread of emergent human infectious diseases and plays a key role in human-mediated bio-invasion, the dominant factor in the global biodiversity crisis. What is less well understood is what the impact of co-infection will be on such control strategies, especially if one infection masks another.

While co-infection models are relatively well studied in influenza epidemics (Colijn et al. 2009) and other related diseases (Keeling 1999), there is still uncertainty as to how such co-infection models can be applied to HIV and related infections. These models may then be useful for extracting parameter values for exposure, susceptibility, and infection that can be used in future preventative strategies to target key co-infection causes that most contribute to the spread of infectious disease.

There have been many mathematical models of single infection, such as HIV/AIDS infection, based on susceptibility (S), infection (I) and recovery (R). However, there has been much less research on co-infection (simultaneous infection by two or more pathogens). It is noted that there have been a growing number of reports discussing HIV and hepatitis C (HCV) co-infection; it appears that HIV-infected individuals are commonly co-infected with HCV, when the transmission and evolution of HIV/AIDS and HCV are a dynamic process.

It is hypothesised that rural deaths will outnumber urban, and the difference will be statistically significant. Infections and deaths will also be significantly different by age. Cases of co-infection between rural and urban and by age will be measured against identified factors mentioned above. The study will provide further insight into factors leading to higher rural and infant death rates and to explore economical and feasible interventions for reducing death and narrowing the infectious-disease gap in co-infection.

Moreover, these studies model the impact of isoniazid preventive therapy (IPT) in controlling the spread of active TB infection amongst inmates in correctional facilities. IPT taken for at least six months is recognised as an effective preventive measure for active TB (World Health Organization 2011). The WHO has also recently introduced a guideline for resource-constrained settings, recommending IPT to be initiated to all HIV-infected persons, irrespective of tuberculin skin test (TST) reactivity (WHO 2011) However, clinical trials suggest that it is more effective amongst those with positive TST results (Akolo et al. 2004, Smieja et al. 2000).

Despite the WHO's recent recommendations and evidence of IPT effectiveness in community settings, the implementation of IPT in correctional facilities is limited, particularly in low- and middle-income countries (LMICs). This might be attributed to concerns about exclusion of active TB, safety of the intervention amongst people with co-morbidities, and about the effectiveness of IPT due to high re-infection rate in a closed setting.

TB has slow intrinsic dynamics. The incubation period, latency period, and infectious period span long intervals, in the order of years on average. The slow progression of TB at the individual level leads to slow temporal dynamics and long-term outcomes of the disease at the population level. Therefore, mathematical models are needed to estimate prolonged results and future trends of tuberculosis.

Several studies on TB-transmission dynamic in a population setting have been conducted using mathematical modelling (Aparicio, et al. 2009; Blower, et al. 1995; Brooks-Pollock, et al. 2010; Cooper-Arnold, et al. 1999; Feng, et al. 2000; Liao, et al. 2012; Ozcaglar, et al. 2012; Rust, et al. 1975; Salpeter, et al. 1998; Viljoen, et al. 2012; Waaler, et al. 1962; Waaler, et al. 1970; White et al. 2010). However, modelling of TB transmission in a closed setting has not been conducted.

In the epidemiology of TB, mathematical modelling has been used as an important tool for policymakers and public-health researchers, who use mathematical models to gain insight into the potential long-term consequences of programmatic decisions (Waaler, et al. 1962).

Finally, this study will investigate how probabilistic parameters affect the model in terms of time, location, gender, age, and subgroups of the population. The outcome will be used to test the effectiveness of education programmes in reducing the number of co-infection cases. Also, the models may give rise to new mathematical principles and different ways to view co-infection from an epidemiological perspective.

It is believed that effective preventative measures for AIDS must take into account the high probability of HCV and TB co-infection if HIV, TB, and HCV are to be controlled. The beneficiaries of this research will be not just the above-mentioned healthcare professionals but also other medical areas where co-infections are prevalent.

Focus of the Chapter

The focus of this chapter is to describe issues and challenges raised in research related to the spread of infectious diseases in two different settings. The first research study will investigate the wide spread of HIV amongst a general population engaging in high-risk behaviour in Ghana. The second research involves a closed-setting environment, looking for the dynamic spread of TB amongst inmates in correctional facilities in Malaysia. In both parts of the research, problematic issues and challenges are addressed using mathematical methods to analyse the data and computational tools for simulation and modelling. This chapter will also describe some recommendations in addressing the issues and challenges raised, as well as to provide some insight for improved future research.

Issues and Challenges

Ethical Issues

Ethical issues might arise while studying infectious diseases' dynamics. It involves a certain structuring of perception, a certain kind of seeing as confidentiality. To see a certain state of affairs or decision as a moral issue is to see that it has significant implications for harms or benefits that human beings experience (Franklin, et al. 2001; Kleijnen 2001). In correctional settings, ethical management is a very complex issue. A research team is bound to adhere to certain legal and regulatory policies and practises that could hamper the quality of research study.

Despite the availability of guidelines that stress the rights of potential research subjects to participate and withdraw at any time during studies, inmates in correctional settings are frequently subjected to many ethical violations in relation to research enrolment. Being an exceptionally vulnerable population, inmates might face penalties or receive disadvantaged treatment from correctional authorities for refusing to participate in studies. These might be in the form of isolation, reducing out-of-cell hours, and restricting them from working in paid prison jobs (in countries where such jobs are offered). These measures, in addition to violating research protocols, might additionally affect the relationship between research team and inmates and consequently add a negative image to the research, causing a general lack of interest in research participation.

The safety and confidentiality of research in correctional settings can be very challenging. Security and surveillance are the central parts of the prison system. The researcher is ethically responsible to protect participants' confidentiality, but often in correctional settings, where security is a major concern, it is almost impossible to warrant confidentiality (UNAIDS 2010). The prison authorities require a security officer to be present at all times when an inmate is involved, to maintain safety for all individuals within the setting. In addition to violating research protocols, the presence of an officer during the interview process creates an uncomfortable atmosphere for participants to answer questions freely, which may jeopardise the accuracy of the collected data.

On the other hand, while most research trials – in particular those related to infectious diseases – are designed to evaluate incidence rates in an active group, in comparison to a control group, the ethical obligation would call for an equal intervention package for both active and control groups to remain uninfected (UNAIDS 2010). This could be addressed by providing a minimum standard of risk-reduction package for both arms. But this also means that the research will require a larger sample size for both arms, to produce a statistically significant outcome. An increase in sample size could cost more money, due to the extension of duration to recruit sufficient enumerators or research assistants to recruit sufficient respondents.

Data and Modelling Issues

Data on HIV infection and other related diseases are poorly characterised in less-developed countries, especially in Asia. Dokubo, et al. (2013) conducted a systematic review of peer-reviewed English-language publications and conference abstracts on HIV incidence in thirteen countries in Asia and found that surveillance systems that routinely monitor trends are needed. Comparative studies are almost impossible, due to a lack of standard available data. In the countries with available data, incidence rates were highest in key populations and varied widely by incidence-estimation method.

Risk factors associated with HIV infections are affected by the place where the studies are conducted or the target groups included in the study. For example, risk factors for incident HIV infection include brothel-based sex work and cervicitis amongst commercial sex workers; young age; frequent injection use and sharing needles or syringes amongst people who inject drugs; multiple male sexual partners, receptive anal intercourse; and syphilis infection amongst men who have sex with men.

In most studies, the sample size of the surveyed groups is small. In many situations, the population's standard deviation is unknown, basically due to various constraints on collecting data challenges, for example, time, cost, and practicality. It is essential for the sample size to be small, since the sample size is part of the fully defined population. To make accurate inferences, the sample size has to be representative. A representative sample size is one in which each and every member of the population has an equal and mutually exclusive chance of being selected. However, a reasonable sample size acceptable in this research will utilise the calculated margin of error.

While co-infection models are relatively well known in influenza literature (Colijn, et al. 2009) and foot-and-mouth infection (Keeling 1999), there is still uncertainty as to how such co-infection models can be applied to HIV and related infections. There have been several mathematical models, which have not taken into account the some important issues. For example, Colijnet, et al. (2009) demonstrated why susceptible-exposed-infective-recovery models can be used to model latent co-infection of tuberculosis with different strains. Drawback: their model did not present how co-infection of TB with a different but associated disease could be modelled. The description of the SIR models are greatly affected by the way in which transmission between infected and susceptible individuals are modelled. Roeger, et al. (2009) formulated a simplified deterministic model of co-infection between TB and HIV. Different independent reproduction numbers were used to represent TB and HIV respectively. While individual-to-individual transmissions are modelled, neither model deals with population migration, one of the key factors in the spread of HIV and HCV, as well as other diseases.

Mathematical modelling of the projected benefit of IPT on TB burden in closed settings is yet to be explored. Our literature search found that previous studies on TB-transmission modelling in a closed setting generally adapted the Wells-Riley equation, which measures the number of new infections based on a fixed number of infectors, but not the full dynamic of the transmission (Chen, et al. 2011; Furuya, et al. 2009; Watase 2005). Chen, et al. (2011) modelled TB transmission amongst passenger in trains; Furuya, et al. (2009) studied a TB transmission model in an Internet cafe; whilst Watase (2005) studied a TB transmission model in an overcrowded school. But Legrand, et al. (2008) successfully demonstrated that a stochastic compartmental model alone in a Rio de Janeiro prison could also estimate the impact of different TB control strategies (DOT, chest X-ray, and smear positive at entry point and annual X-ray screening).

In 2006, Noakes, et al. developed a general model for airborne infections in a confined setting, based on the Wells-Riley equation, incorporated with compartmental epidemic model. The model was developed with consideration of a short incubation period to stimulate the transmission dynamic of airborne infectious disease in indoor environments such as hospitals. Another study by Basu et al. (2007) and Basu et al. (2009) adapted the Wells-Riley equation, combined with a compartmental system, to model the TB transmission as the infected person moved between disease states and environments.

Logistic and Structural Barrier

One of the most important first tasks of research is to identify and clearly define the problem or develop a research question an individual wishes to study. Almost all research is set in motion by the existence of a problem. A problem is defined as a difficulty, a discrepancy between what someone believes should be the situation and what the reality of the situation is. However, at the beginning of any research, there is a force of problem behind it; not all problems require research. Any potential research situation arises when these three conditions exist:

1. Is there perceived discrepancy between what is and what should be?
2. Is there a question about why there is a discrepancy?
3. Are there at least two possible and plausible answers to the question?

The last point is very important. If there is only one possible and plausible answer to the question about the discrepancy, then a research situation does not exist.

Funding support could be one of the major factors affecting research implementation. These include allocation of staff, incentives for participants, facility, transportation, equipment, and tools. In our experience, working with a large sample of respondents, allocation of some incentives resulted in higher follow-up rates and increased willingness to participate in future research. Although there was a debate on whether giving incentives could cause unnecessary inducement such as repeat enrolment, this can be addressed through compensating them with an appropriate scale of incentives during recruitment and follow-up (UNAIDS 2010). However, limitation in funding might force the research team to opt for lower incentives. A facility with a lack of equipment and tools due to lack of funding could also cause interruption and delays in research. Delays in research even cost more money to pay for the salaries of staff, utilities, and rental.

Human resources in research are essential to execute collection and management of data, as well as the primary contact between respondents and the research team. The position is generally known as enumerators or research assistants, of whom a majority are fresh graduates with bachelor's degrees. In our research experience, the high turnover amongst enumerators or research assistants could become an issue during the data-collection process. The coordinator of the research team needs to invest time and energy to look for a new research assistant and provide necessary training. The new personnel will need time to learn and familiarise themselves with the research background. Some may decide to resign halfway through if the research theme is not of interest or they have a lack of understanding and acceptance, in particular when working around sensitive issues such as our research.

In an environment where stigma and discrimination still prevail amongst a marginalised population, finding the right committed human resources could be challenging.

Additionally, participation in research studies inside prisons might disrupt the everyday life of inmates. Waiting for long hours, delays in meal supply, reduction in sport/outside-activity hours, and lost paid-work days are perceived examples. Research outcomes add an additional burden on research subjects, particularly when subjects are diagnosed with infectious diseases, including HIV and tuberculosis. Stigma, segregation, and prolonged isolation may have an impact on inmates' interest in participation in related research studies.

The coexistence of punitive policies targeting people who use drugs and health policy remain critical barriers for study implementation (Kamarulzaman 2009). Strict anti-drug laws, regulations, and enforcement procedures expose drug users to fines or imprisonment, impose mandatory registration and reporting duties, and drive drug users underground, thus creating a hidden and hard-to-reach population. In turn, these can influence people's willingness to participate in prevention trials, hamper researchers' recruitment efforts, and affect the willingness of those already enrolled in trials to utilise risk-reduction and treatment-referral services.

Research Bias

This section will pay particular attention on how to minimise issues and challenges pertaining to network modelling of the spread of infectious disease. One significant class of errors is known as bias. Bias, as defined in epidemiology, is any systemic error that results in an incorrect estimate of the association between exposure and disease (Rothman, et al. 2008). Bias can also occur in randomised controlled trials, though it tends to be a much greater problem in observational studies (Lewis-Beck, et al. 2004). To understand the nature of bias, we need to establish that exposure to a particular risk factor contributes to a health problem of infectious disease. The main types of bias included in the modelling of infectious diseases are selection, information, recall, and confounding.

Selection bias usually occurs when there is no random sampling drawn from the population being studied (Sica 2006). Information bias occurs when there are systematic differences in the way surveillance data on exposure or outcome are derived from the different study groups (Hennekens, et al. 1987). Recall bias occurs in a case control study where the reporting of the disease state is different depending on the exposure state. Confounding bias arises when additional factors or variables are associated with both exposure and, independently, with disease status, and these additional factors have a mixed effect (Gerhard 2008).

The earlier-mentioned issues and the challenges can be minimised in the following ways:

1. Find the proportion of people in a population who are exposed to the risk factor.
2. Find the proportions of people in a population who either, having been exposed to risk factor or not unexposed, later develop the infectious disease.

3. Find the association between the risk factor and the infectious
    disease.

These proportions would be addressed in future research studies.
For example, a mathematical model will be formulated based on the
nature of the outcome of the experimental work performed by the
researcher.

The fit of mathematical models to surveillance data has bias
estimation of parameters involved. This has led to difficulty issues,
informed in both scientific research and health-policy makers. The
challenge of modelling the most devastating and intractable of
infectious diseases can only be achieved through a concerted and multi-
institutional effort. The scientific and technological competence requires
mathematicians working on infectious-disease modelling, public-health
researchers, and public employees engaged with the logistical realities
of disease control. We need to foster a productive interchange that will
hopefully lead to substantial progress in the development of control
strategies for preventive measures. These research biases can be avoided
by taking into account careful consideration and controlling the ways
in which bias may be introduced during the design of the study.

Other Challenges

A strong working collaboration with stakeholders, in particular
dealing with a marginalised population, plays an important role in
research. The translation of research findings into an action plan
depends on stakeholders' interests. The main challenges generally
encountered with stakeholders are related to their perspective to
health research. Health-research studies are perceived as an additional,
unnecessary burden on security officers. Mobilisations of a large

number of prisoners, escorting research teams, and proximity of research materials to dangerous inmates were reported frequently by security officers as major security concerns.

On another issue, there might be some conflicting issues between correctional officers and health staff. Prison officers might inflict certain measures in line with their security orientation, including prevention of inmates' mobilisation or prolonged security checks. Additionally, these measures might restrict health researchers from accessing some research subjects.

Conclusion and Future Research

In this section, we explore the implications of extending the ideas from the issues and the challenges outlined to develop a mathematical model from a theoretical perspective; however, the following research issues would be addressed:

- There have been several mathematical models – one of the key factors in the spread of infectious disease, as well as other diseases – although individual-to-individual transmission is modelled.

There is very little understanding of how HIV, TB, and HCV, and other major co-infection diseases, are related in mathematical terms. Moreover, three main issues and challenges have been outlined in section 2.4: firstly, the proportion of people in a population who are exposed to risk factor; secondly, the proportions of people in a population who either, having been exposed to risk factor or not unexposed, later develop the infectious disease; and finally, the association between the risk factor and infectious disease.

Recommendations/Suggestions

Based on issues and challenges discussed in this chapter, the following are some of the recommendations and suggestions which can be adopted in implementing infectious-disease research, for example in HIV, TB, and hepatitis C.

- Solid education programmes for both inmates and prison officers need to be established to tackle research-study barriers. These programmes need to highlight the importance of conducting health-related research studies on the health of inmates, security officers, and their families, and the community at large.
- Protocols for research in prisons and other closed settings must give due consideration to issues of voluntariness of consent; strategies for the protection of confidentiality and safety of participants; access to risk-reduction packages; monitoring, management, and reporting of adverse events (e.g., availability of medical care and access to such care after hours); and responsibilities to report abuses in prisons.
- Where studies are conducted inside prisons and other closed settings, researchers should make plans to assist participants in the transition to the community and to address the known increased risks of injecting and sexual behaviour, intimate-partner violence, and opioid overdose upon release from detention.
- Consultation with prospective participants prior to the research may facilitate in determining the amount and form of remuneration. The remuneration could be in the form of conditional cash transfers, whereby participants are paid for

performing or abstaining from certain actions or for obtaining certain outcomes. Consultation prior to research could improve acceptability of the study and maximizing recruitment and retention.

References

Akolo, C, et al. (2004). "Treatment of Latent Tuberculosis Infection in HIV-Infected Persons". *Cochrane Database of Systematic Reviews Online*, CD000171.

Al-Darraji, H A A, Kamarulzaman, A, and F L Altice (2012). "Isoniazid Preventive Therapy in Correctional Facilities: A Systematic Review" [Review article]. *Int J Tuberc Lung Dis*, 16, 871–879.

Aparicio, J P, and C Castillo-Chavez (2009). "Mathematical Modelling of Tuberculosis Epidemics". *Math Biosci Eng*, 6, 209–237.

Basu, S, et al. (2007). "Prevention of Nosocomial Transmission of Extensively Drug-Resistant Tuberculosis in Rural South African District Hospitals: An Epidemiological Modelling Study". *Lancet*, 370 (9597), 1500–1507.

Basu, S, Maru, D, Poolman, E, and A Galvani (2009). "Primary and Secondary Tuberculosis Preventive Treatment in HIV Clinics: Simulating Alternative Strategies. *Int J Tuberc Lung Dis*, 13 (5), 652–658.

Baussano, I, et al. (2010). "Tuberculosis Incidence in Prisons: A Systematic Review". *PLoS Medicine*, 7, e1000381.

Blower, S M, et al. (1995). "The Intrinsic Transmission Dynamics of Tuberculosis Epidemics". *Nat Med*, 1, 815–821.

Brooks-Pollock, E, Cohen, T, and M Murray (2010). "The Impact of Realistic Age Structure in Simple Models of Tuberculosis Transmission". *PLoS One*, 5, e8479.

Chen, S-C, Liao, C-M, Li, S-S, and S-H You (2011). "A Probabilistic Transmission Model to Assess Infection Risk from Mycobacterium Tuberculosis in Commercial Passenger Trains". *Risk Analysis: An Official Publication of the Society for Risk Analysis*, 31, 930–939.

Colijn, C, Cohen, T, and M Murray (2009). "Latent Coinfection and the Maintenance of Strain Diversity". *Bulletin of Mathematical Biology* (71), 247–263.

Cooper-Arnold, K, et al. (1999). "Occupational Tuberculosis Among Deputy Sheriffs in Connecticut: A Risk Model of Transmission". *Appl Occup Environ Hyg,* 14, 768–776.

Dokubo, E K, et al. (2013). "HIV Incidence in Asia: A Review of Available Data and Assessment of the Epidemic. *AIDS Review,* 15(2), 67–76.

Feng, Z, Castillo-Chavez, C, and A F Capurro (2000). "A Model for Tuberculosis with Exogenous Reinfection". *Theoretical Population Biology,* 57, 235–247.

Franklin, G M, and C Grady (2001). "The Ethical Challenge of Infection-Inducing Challenge Experiments". *Clinical Infectious Diseases,* 33 (7), 1028–1033.

Furuya, H, Nagamine, M, and T Watanabe (2009). "Use of a Mathematical Model to Estimate Tuberculosis Transmission Risk in an Internet Cafe". *Environmental Health and Preventive Medicine,* 14, 96–102.

Gerhard, T (2008). "Bias: Considerations for Research Practice". *Research Fundamentals,* 65, 2159–2168.

Hennekens, C, and J Buring (1987). *Epidemiology in Medicine.* Boston: Little, Brown.

Kamarulzaman, A (2009). "Impact of HIV Prevention Programs on Drug Users in Malaysia". *Journal of Acquired Immune Deficiency Syndromes,* Volume 52, 17–19.

Keeling, M J (1999). "The Effects of Local Spatial Structure on Epidemiological Invasions". *Proceedings of the Royal Society of London B,* 266, 859–867.

Kleijnen, J P C (2001). "Ethical Issues in Modeling: Some Reflections". *European Journal of Operational Research,* 130 (1), 223–230.

Lewis-Beck, M S, Bryman, A, and T F Liao (2004). *The SAGE Encyclopedia of Social Science Research Methods.* SAGE Publications, Inc.

Liao, C M, et al. (2012). "A Probabilistic Transmission and Population Dynamic Model to Assess Tuberculosis Infection Risk". *Risk Anal,* 32, 1420–1432.

Moller, L, Gatherer, A, and M Dara (2009). "Barriers to Implementation of Effective Tuberculosis Control in prisons". *Public Health, 123,* 419–421.

Noakes, C J, Beggs, C B, Sleigh, P A, and K G Kerr (2006). "Modelling the Transmission of Airborne Infections in Enclosed Spaces". *Epidemiol Infect,* 134 (5), 1082–1091.

Ozcaglar, C, et al. (2012). "Epidemiological Models of Mycobacterium Tuberculosis Complex Infections". *Mathematical Biosciences, 236,* 77–96.

Pawlowski, A, et al. (2012). "Tuberculosis and HIV Co-Infection". *PLoS pathogens,* 8, e1002464.

Roeger, L I, Feng, Z, and C Castillo-Chavez (2009). "Modeling TB and HIV Co-Infections". *Math Biosci Eng,* 6, 815-837.

Rothman, K, Greenland, S, and T Lash (2008). *Modern Epidemiology.* Lipincott Williams and Wilkins, Philadephia.

Rust, P and J Thomas (1975). "A Method for Estimating the Prevalence of Tuberculosis Infection". *Am J Epidemiol,* 101, 311–322.

Salpeter, E E, and S R Salpeter (1998). "Mathematical Model for the Epidemiology of Tuberculosis, with Estimates of the Reproductive Number and Infection-Delay Function". *Am J Epidemiol,* 147, 398–406.

Selwyn, P A, et al. (1989). "A Prospective Study of the Risk of Tuberculosis among Intravenous Drug Users with Human Immunodeficiency Virus Infection". *The New England Journal of Medicine,* 320 (9), 545–550.

Sica, G T (2006). "Bias in Research Studies". *Radiology* (238), 780–789.

Smieja, M J, Marchetti, C A, Cook, D J, and F M Smaill (2000). "Isoniazid for Preventing Tuberculosis in Non-HIV Infected Persons". *Cochrane Database of Systematic Reviews Online,* 1, CD001363.

The *PLoS Medicine* Editors (2010). The Health Crisis of Tuberculosis in Prisons Extends beyond the Prison Walls. PLoS Med 7(12): e1000383. doi:10.1371/journal.pmed.1000383.

UNAIDS (2010). *Ethical Engagement of People Who Inject Drugs in HIV Prevention Trials.* Geneva, Switzerland.

Viljoen, S, Pienaar, E, and H J Viljoen (2012). "A State-Time Epidemiology Model of Tuberculosis: Importance of Re-Infection". *Comput Biol Chem,* 36, 15–22.

Waaler, H, Geser, A, and S Andersen (1962). "The Use of Mathematical Models in the Study of the Epidemiology of Tuberculosis". *Am J Public Health Nations Health,* 52, 1002–1013.

Waaler, H T and M A Piot (1970). "Use of an Epidemiological Model for Estimating the Effectiveness of Tuberculosis Control Measures. Sensitivity of the Effectiveness of Tuberculosis Control Measures to the Social Time Preference". *Bull World Health Organ,* 43, 1–16.

Watase, H (2005). "The Transmission of Tuberculosis in a Cram School". *Kekkaku Tuberculosis,* 80, 461–467.

White, P J, and G P Garnett (2010). "Mathematical Modelling of the Epidemiology of Tuberculosis". *Adv Exp Med Biol,* 673, 127–140.

World Health Organization (2000). *Tuberculosis Control in Prisons: A Manual for Programme Managers.*

———— (2011). "Guidelines for Intensified Tuberculosis Case-Finding and Isoniazid Preventive Therapy for People Living with HIV in Resource-Constrained Settings". *World Health,* 01, 187.

———— (2012). *Global Tuberculosis Report 2012.* Paper presented at the WHO, Geneva, Switzerland.